IN THE

— MY LIFE —

BLACK

B. DENHAM JOLLY

Published by ECW Press
665 Gerrard Street East
Toronto, ON M4M 1Y2
416-694-3348 / info@ecwpress.com

Cover design: Tania Craan
Cover and interior images courtesy of the author
Author photo: Fitzroy Facey
Type: Rachel Ironstone

Printing: Friesens   1   2   3   4   5

To the best of his abilities, the author has related
experiences, places, people, and organizations from his
memories of them. In order to protect the privacy of
others, he has, in some instances, changed the names of
certain people and details of events and places

Library and Archives Canada
Cataloguing in Publication

Jolly, B. Denham, author
In the black : my life / B. Denham Jolly.

Issued in print and electronic formats.
ISBN 978-1-77041-378-8 (hardback)
ISBN 978-1-77090-994-6 (PDF)
ISBN 978-1-77090-993-9 (ePub)

1. Jolly, B. Denham. 2. Flow FM (Radio station: Toronto,
Ont.)—Biography. 3. Jamaican Canadians—Biography.
4. Blacks—Canada—Social conditions. 5. Black
Canadians—Ontario—Toronto—Biography. 6. Business
enterprises, Black—Ontario—Toronto—Biography.
7. Radio stations—Ontario—Toronto. I. Title.

HE8699.C2J65 2017   384.5406'5713541   C2016-906349-6
C2016-906350-X

The publication of *In the Black* has been generously supported by the Canada Council for the Arts, which last year invested
$153 million to bring the arts to Canadians throughout the country, and by the Government of Canada through the Canada
Book Fund. *Nous remercions le Conseil des arts du Canada de son soutien. L'an dernier, le Conseil a investi 153 millions de dollars
pour mettre de l'art dans la vie des Canadiennes et des Canadiens de tout le pays. Ce livre est financé en partie par le gouvernement
du Canada.* We also acknowledge the support of the Ontario Arts Council (OAC), an agency of the Government of
Ontario, which last year funded 1,737 individual artists and 1,095 organizations in 223 communities across Ontario for a
total of $52.1 million, and the contribution of the Government of Ontario through the Ontario Book Publishing Tax Credit
and the Ontario Media Development Corporation.

Printed and bound in Canada

To my grandson
Elias James Jolly Klym
Who has brought new joy and meaning to my life.

CONTENTS

IN THE

BLACK

CHAPTER ONE
IN THE LION'S DEN

When you are Black in Canada, the arrival of the police on the scene is not always, or even often, reassuring.

Three years ago, on Parliament Street in Toronto's Cabbagetown neighbourhood, not far from where I live, I had a fender bender. I was exchanging insurance information with the other driver when a police officer came to take charge of the situation. There was nothing really for him to do, but he told me that I should call a tow truck to get my car towed away.

I told him, very politely, that it wasn't a problem. The car was only dented, and I could easily drive it to a garage. But he insisted.

When I balked, he immediately escalated. "You have to get a tow truck," he said.

I found this incomprehensible — towing a car away when it only had a dent. But the officer looked at me contemptuously.

"What do I have to do to make sure you do, put a gun in your face?"

For a moment, I could not believe my ears. A threat like that, made almost casually on a busy Toronto street. I was in my late seventies and my first thought was, what if I had been a Black kid in his twenties? Would he have threatened to draw his gun or have simply done so? Far too often in Toronto's recent history that had been the case, and dozens of Black kids had been killed that way.

That thought angered me, but I was not seeking a confrontation. I said nothing. I called the tow truck.

But I did not want to let the matter pass. I filed an official complaint with the department. I made it clear that I wasn't asking that the officer be fired but that he receive some kind of counselling to address his threatening behaviour before someone was hurt.

At first, the department brushed aside my complaint with the excuse that the officer was already in trouble for other indiscretions and he was about to be charged. This turned out to be untrue. I pursued my case as far as I could, but it was clear the Toronto police department wasn't interested in dealing with it. I complained and appealed all the way to the chief of police, Bill Blair.

The department's investigation showed that the officer had his body speaker turned off during the confrontation. They believed him when he denied saying those words. The verdict was clear. "We can't substantiate your claim." End of story.

I did get to see the police report, however, and the opening phrase told me everything I needed to know about what was behind the incident. The report began with, "The complainant, a seventy-seven-year-old Jamaican immigrant . . ."

At the time, I had lived in Canada more than fifty-five years, longer than the officer had been alive, and I had been a citizen for almost fifty years. If I had been a white man, my origins would have been irrelevant. But a Black man, by definition, had to be identified as the "other," not as someone who had been a Canadian for half a century. I was forever a "Jamaican immigrant." That is why he could threaten to put a gun in my face and then lie about it.

Who would believe a Jamaican immigrant?

Part of my story is about Canada's uncomfortable struggle with Blackness, which I experienced that day on Parliament Street and on thousands of other occasions. This is a reality in Canada. Even though the first Black in Canada, Mathieu da Costa, arrived with Samuel de Champlain in 1603, Blacks were prevented from settling in Canada in any great numbers until well into the 1970s and that legacy of exclusion continues today.

I arrived on a student visa two decades before the immigration gates were opened to any degree. I am today, even though I visit Jamaica often, thoroughly Canadian. But I hope I will not disappoint my white Canadian friends, of which I am happy to have many, when I say I am not one of those who unrelentingly sing the praises of my adopted country. Despite meeting many nice people, I discovered when I arrived in Canada that it was an unapologetically and insistently white country with a tiny Black minority kept at a fairly steady .02% of the population and largely assigned to jobs as domestics (for women) and railway porters (for men). Things have improved, of course, and the fight to make a better Canada is part of the story I am telling here, but Canada still has a distance to go before it lives up to its ideals.

This is a story of progress made, as well as the challenges remaining. My journey is the journey of a Jamaican who left his country at the age of twenty and who has been part of the evolution in Canada since 1955. Now, as I have entered my eightieth year, I would like to lay down a record of my personal experiences and recount something of the Black struggle in Canada in the last half of the twentieth century and the beginning of the twenty-first. Along the way, I would like to introduce readers, Black and white, to some remarkable women and men that I have had the privilege of knowing and often fighting alongside over the past many decades. These Black Canadians are important for our people to know because they are part of our inspiring legacy in this country. They are important for white people to know because they worked, often in opposition to governments and enforcement bodies, to make Canada a better, more just country. This is an opportunity for you to get to know them, and for the white reader to better get to know Black Canada.

This, I believe, is essential if we are truly to build a harmonious society together. You'll notice, though, that I do not say "get to know each other." Because the fact is, we Black Canadians already know white Canada very well. We have to. We know you the same way that the hare knows the lion, from following its every move. And for the same reason. Because in certain circumstances, you can be dangerous to us. My hope is that when you, the white reader, let yourself know us in a more profound way, you will become a little more human and a little less the lion in your dealings with us.

So I welcome all of you, Black and white and all my brothers and sisters of other races, to accompany me on my journey into our collective past. My story is largely a Canadian one because it is in Canada where I built a life, first as a student, then as a high school teacher, and finally as a businessman and media owner and activist. But it begins in a little village in Hanover Parish in Jamaica at a time when Britannia still ruled the waves and most of our small blue planet.

CHAPTER TWO

GROWING UP BRITISH
IN INDUSTRY COVE

As it turned out, the Empire would even be involved in my naming.

It was August 26, 1935, and my mother was lying in labour with her second child in an upstairs room in our house. Someone had already sent for the doctor, but he had not yet arrived, and my father was waiting nervously on the side of the road when a passing labourer told him that the newly appointed British governor was touring the Island; that afternoon, he was scheduled to drive through Industry Cove, our hamlet in Hanover Parish just north of the town of Green Island. My father, Benjamin Augustus Jolly, was already in his mid-fifties. He was far from a British loyalist. In fact, he was not really interested in politics at all, but for some reason, perhaps to kill time while he waited for news of my birth, he decided to look around for a Union Jack to fly from the flagpole near the road where the new governor would be passing. If nothing else, this simple act would kill another half an hour while he waited for the results of my mother's labour.

But this unpremeditated act had unintended consequences. When Sir Edward Brandis Denham drove by in his open car and spotted the flag, he ordered the driver to stop so he could get out and greet the person who'd raised it. Our region had a reputation for unrest among the interior sugar estate workers, and Sir Edward must have felt that this symbol of loyalty should not go unrewarded. My father was probably caught off guard by the governor's gesture, but they exchanged pleasantries.

Sir Edward was a moderately impressive man. A career imperial bureaucrat, he had served as governor of the Gambia and British Guiana before his Jamaican posting. He was known well enough in the Empire to have his own cigarette card in the Ardath Tobacco Company *Empire Personalities* series (he was card forty-nine of fifty; George VI was number one). I can't imagine that my father would have much to say to him, and I don't know if he mentioned that he was awaiting the birth of his second child, but after a few minutes, the governor headed on his way to Lucea, where he would meet with the officials of our parish. News of his visit was carried up to my mother, Ina Euphemia Jolly (née Arthurs), who was enduring a long labour. It obviously made an impression on her because when I was finally born later that day, she decided to name me after this chance meeting between her husband and the governor.

So I became Brandeis Denham Jolly. Three years later I became the only Brandeis Denham on the Island when the governor, whose administration continued to be plagued by strikes and uprisings by the sugar workers, died suddenly of a heart attack in the splendour of King's House in Kingston.

His last name, Denham, is remembered in Jamaica today mainly for Denham Town, a neighbourhood in west-central Kingston known as one of the city's most violent. But the Brandeis Denham Jolly name has served me well. It is unusual enough that people tend to remember me for it but it still also allows for more familiar variations, like Denny, which is what I was called when I was growing up in Jamaica in the late 1930s and early 1940s, and what many of my friends call me today.

There is no question that I had a happy childhood. Part of this might have been due to the position of my family at the time. My father's side of the family owned 300 acres of land in and around Green Island, which, despite its name, was not an island but a coastal town. And my father, who was twenty years older than my mother, was a local entrepreneur involved in all sorts of money-making ventures. At various times, he owned a grocery store, a bar, and a bakery with a hand-operated mill that made a locally famous hard dough bread, as well as buns and peg bread. He even owned a small fleet of bread vans, both mule drawn and motorized, that delivered to neighbouring districts. At various times, my father also ran a trucking enterprise, as well as growing coconuts, bananas, sugar cane, and other cash crops on our lands. We were never hungry and never had to stay home from school for lack of tuition money. We lived in a part of the country that didn't have electricity until the 1950s, so my father gained a bit of local notoriety when he purchased the first automobile in the area in the '40s.

My father, Benjamin Augustus Jolly.

He was proud of his business talent. He had made his own way in the world. He had begun his working life as a cooper at the Prospect Sugar Factory three miles away, making barrels for rum. He worked hard, saved, and invested. When I was young, people called him "Cappy" Jolly, short for "Capital," and I heard him several times reminding his employees, "But on payday I hold my hand like this," showing the giving gesture, "while you hold your hand like this," turning his palm up in the taking gesture. In his career advice to me, he said: "Don't work for anyone but yourself. And always own property."

For my father, these two principles suited both his talents and his nature, and they gave us a comfortable existence. Still, even as children, we were expected to work through the day. My brother and sisters and I were wakened at dawn every morning by my father, and we were expected to take care of the livestock and fetch water before going to school.

Those were, of course, much simpler times for everyone. Without electricity, light in the evening came from flickering coal-oil lamps. My father did have a battery-powered radio, but batteries were so scarce that it was rarely played. He turned it on only for the news and for international cricket matches. Music was played on our own instruments, especially the piano in the living room, which my mother played very well.

My mother made sure we were always well dressed, and my father had a kind of elegance in his person. His hobby was the gentleman's pursuit of racing horses. He had a stable with riding and racing horses, and he would go riding on our lands dressed like a country squire in jodhpurs, riding boots, and spurs. To feed them, he bought corn that he ground on the bakery hand mill. My older sister, Barbara, remembers that "Dada," as we called him, was always on his horse when he wasn't driving his car. On weekends, he would race his horses at the Fairfield race track in Montego Bay.

Although my father did not have a strong interest in politics, he did have a strong sense of community responsibility. The only well in the district was on his property, and he welcomed villagers onto our land for free access to our water. On major holidays, he would butcher a goat or a cow and put on a barbecue and invite the whole village. He was guided by the unspoken *noblesse oblige*, requiring those who had more to give more. That was the way things worked in Jamaica, and it helped even things out.

My mother was equally industrious and had a creative touch. She designed and produced women's hats and sold them locally. In the kitchen, she made excellent pastries.

Along with playing piano in the parlour, she played the organ at the local Anglican church. (For a time I was an altar boy there, but it didn't last. I did not like being stuck inside on those sunny Sunday mornings.) My mother was a woman who believed strongly in education, and she pushed us to study. This was made easier because she rented rooms to two teachers at the

My mother, Ina Euphemia Jolly (née Arthurs).

school. Ms. Chambers and Mme. Lewellyn were wonderful women. They were like members of the family, and they often tutored us in their free time.

My mother, known as Miss Ina to most people, insisted we behave with proper decorum — no elbows on the table — and observe the basic rules of etiquette. She wanted to make sure that no doors would be closed to us. Meals were always a special time. Food was cooked in an outdoor kitchen, then brought to the pantry and placed into serving dishes. The table was always set with a white damask tablecloth, and we all sat down to eat as a family along with boarders and visitors, who were treated as family.

Perhaps most importantly, I learned from my mother that people are not, finally, judged by what they earn or by what position they attain, but by what they give to others. She was always ready to feed the hungry and ensure that the homeless had shelter, and she took in many people, especially children. She was enormously respected in our region, and in later years she was made a local justice of the peace.

We were also a close extended family. We visited my maternal grandmother, Dinah Richards, in Montego Bay several times a year; later, when I went to school there, I would live with her. My paternal grandmother, Angela McKenzie, lived just across the bay in a stone-and-wood two-story house, and when my mother was giving birth to the younger children, we older ones would stay with my grandmother for weeks on end.

Growing up in Industry Cove was a relatively carefree existence. We swam in the sea and fished from the jutting rocks along the shore and often cooked our catch on the beach on driftwood fires. We made slingshots with rubber cut from old tires and hunted birds with them. The local cricket field was on my father's extended lands, and we played endless hours of cricket using young sour oranges as balls and coconut boughs shaped into cricket bats. There were five children in our family, and most other families were of a similar size, so there were always plenty of kids around to play with, and many local and visiting teams came to play on our grounds, something my father welcomed.

In Hanover Parish, we were almost all Blacks, with a few Chinese families, a number of mixed race, and a few white kids. Growing up, we did not make a big deal of the differences between us (although Jamaica did have a complex racial system that I will describe later).

My mother adopted Mary, standing here in front of my family home.

Along with her own children, my mother played a role in raising many other children of the parish. When families were in crisis, their children would mysteriously appear at our dinner table and some would stay with us for considerable lengths of time. She would mother them equally as her own, making sure that they ate properly, minded their manners, and did their homework. Over time, more than a dozen local children shared our family life with us. No fuss was ever made of this generosity on her part. In fact, it was never mentioned. It was simply what you did when you had enough — you shared with others.

When I was between the ages of five and ten, the Empire was at war. In Jamaica, the first thing the governor did when war was declared was clamp down on the unions and put activists in jail under the Defence of the Realm Act. Then they regulated the prices of all commodities to prevent profiteering based on the wartime shortages on items like butter and oil. Immediately after that, Jamaican troops, the Home Guard, began appearing on local beaches with binoculars to search the sea lanes for signs of German U-boat activity. We kids would join the soldiers watching the sea for distant movements on the horizon, and we became quite prolific at spotting real or imagined U-boats.

Another pastime was visiting the Green Island docks, which were always busy with the comings and goings of the local fishermen, and with larger schooners — loaded with sugar and bananas from industrial sugar estates and rusty old hulls — loading corn and tobacco for shipment to Florida and Britain. During the war, there were also numerous Royal Navy, U.S., and Canadian naval ships and patrol boats taking on fresh water and supplies in order to continue their cat-and-mouse hunt for U-boats.

This game was most intense between 1941 and 1943 when it seemed, with the U-boat wreaking havoc on the supply convoys, that Britain was on the brink of collapse. There was special concern in my household for my uncle, a tough little guy with the nickname "Wrought Iron," who was overseas as an artillery gunner. It was one of my jobs to ride my bicycle into the village to get the mail and the *Jamaican Gleaner*, the local newspaper, and our family, like everyone around us, followed the daily progress of the war in its pages. I was too young to read the paper, but the dramatic war photos and the obvious concern of adults around me made an impression. The *Gleaner* was our lifeline to the world, and for many years after moving to Canada to attend university, I would inadvertently refer to all newspapers as the *Gleaner*.

With shipping devoted to the war effort, imported foods were in short supply. Flour was severely rationed, so people had to improvise. Breadfruit was sliced and put in the sun to dry for a day, then pounded and mixed with what little flour we had to make dumplings.

Petrol was rationed, too, so my father spent less time in his car and more on his horse. Automotive parts were also in extremely short supply, and after he had his car and delivery trucks cannibalized at night several times, he started to go out before bed and fire a shot over his parked delivery trucks to warn any potential thieves lurking in the bushes not to tread any closer.

In 1943, Alexander Bustamante, a labour activist imprisoned under the Defence of the Realm Act, was released and founded the Jamaica Labour Party. "Busta," as he was known, was a giant of a man politically — and, at six foot five, physically — and he would soon emerge as a dominant force in the country. This hero was also a local: he had grown up about four miles from our village, and he used to bring his horses down to our beach to wash them in the sea.

As I grew older, this same chore — cooling and washing my father's horses in the ocean — became one of my favourites. I would take them from the stable behind the house to the beach in the afternoons. Riding them down and back was always a thrill, especially when it involved my father's lead racehorse, Ben Hur, who I would open up into full gallop. This was not the choppy bounce you get when trotting; when a racehorse unwinds, it feels as if you are flying.

With so much else going on, I tended to hurry through my academic work, especially since the curriculum was thoroughly and unrelentingly British. In the Green Island public school, we learned British history — all about Oliver Cromwell and the roundheads, the oratory of William Pitt the Younger, and the grandeur of the Victorian age — and nothing at all about Marcus Garvey, who had grown up just up the coast from us to become one of the most important Jamaican political philosophers and international leaders of the twentieth century.

It is impossible to understand the twentieth century Black movement, and my later life in Toronto, without understanding Marcus Garvey.

Garvey was born in 1887 in Saint Ann's Bay, on the north coast, about 90 kilometres east of Montego Bay. After spending a few years working as a journalist in Central America, then a couple of years more of schooling in philosophy and law in London, Garvey returned to Jamaica in 1914 to launch the Universal Negro Improvement Association (UNIA), which promoted a very direct form of Black nationalism. UNIA grew rapidly in Jamaica, and the first international division was formed in New York in

May 1917. Within a month, the organization had two million members all over the United States. By 1920, the UNIA had 1,100 chapters in forty countries around the world, including the U.K., Cuba, Panama, Costa Rica, and Ghana. By 1926, its membership had grown to over eleven million.

Garvey could fill Madison Square Garden with enthusiastic followers almost at will. Modern Black history in North America, from Black power to the Back-to-Africa movement, would have been unthinkable without Garvey's rousing Black nationalism in the first half of the century. More than anything, Garvey offered dignity and proud defiance to people whom individual and institutional racism had been designed to crush. After colonialism almost crumpled us into the ground, Garvey appeared, telling us what we already knew in our hearts: enough was enough. It was time to stand up and demand our rights.

Garvey spent much of the '20s and '30s in the U.S., but he still managed to launch activities around the world: from the transatlantic Black Star Steamship Line in 1919 to his petition of the Negro race presented to the League of Nations in Geneva in 1928, which outlined the worldwide abuse of Africans, to the creation of the People's Political Party in Jamaica in 1929. He died in London in 1940 and was mourned by Blacks around the world, but the organizations he founded continued to have influence for decades. That is why it is so remarkable, and so telling, that Garvey was completely excluded from our British school curriculum. Colonialism, I would come to understand, only remembers what it wants to remember. Ironically, it would only be at a kitchen table in a Toronto rooming house run by a

Jamaican expat that I would come to know and understand the teachings and the importance of Garvey.

It is not surprising that most of us found it impossible to identify with the white British history that we were taught in Jamaica at that time. I valued school mostly for the sporting activities — soccer, cricket, cross-country running — rather than the contents of our books. Still, I performed well enough on the academic side, and I was generally well behaved. The only time I received the strap was when I was kicking the ball in the classroom and knocked a porcelain inkwell off a desk, making a major mess.

But the world, I discovered, could change in an instant. I remember on an early May afternoon riding my bike to the post office to pick up the mail. While I was there, I was told that the news had just come over the telegraph from Europe. The war was over. The British and Allies had won. This was announced to me breathlessly, and that is how I reported it. Pedalling home as fast as I could to tell my family, I shouted to everyone I saw: "The war is over. We won!"

After the war, my Industry Cove life slowly began to expand. I was twelve years old when my grandmother took me to Kingston. It was my first time on the train, which we caught in Montego Bay for the slow trip southeast toward the capital. It was a fascinating journey, full of wonders. I remember sitting by the window and sticking my head out and receiving a faceful of coal dust from the coal wagon behind the engine. The train stopped often and the conductors called the name of the current and next stations in almost lyrical tones as the food sellers rushed to the windows to sell the passengers fruit and sweets. It was like a moving drama, a pageant, a procession through the countryside, and it was the beginning of my discovery of the outside world.

Kingston, at the end of the line, was a revelation. A bustling city of light and noise with tram cars and traffic snarls directed by colonial traffic police wearing white pith helmets and white gloves. So different from Industry Cove and Green Island, which had changed little since the nineteenth century. Now I knew that there was an exciting world out there beyond Hanover Parish, and when I returned home I found myself drawn to it and dreaming about it.

There were other changes at home. In 1947, my mother became the first woman justice of the peace in Hanover. She tried cases in the petty sessions court, signed documents for the police relating to bail for prisoners, wrote letters for citizens, signed applications for passports, and was a member of the panel of lay magistrates for the juvenile court. It was not unusual for her to answer a call after midnight to grant bail — as an act of compassion and mercy — to someone who had been arrested during the night, allowing them to leave the jail. She was also one of the rare justices of the peace who didn't charge people for simply signing documents or giving references.

Very soon I would find myself leaving my Industry Cove home. There was no high school in our village, and in 1948, my mother sent me to Montego Bay, where my maternal grandmother lived and my older sister was also staying, to Cornwall College, the all boys high school there. Even though my father was skeptical about this, my mother knew that the best thing she could arm her children with in life was a good education. In the end, all of her children would owe her a great gift of gratitude for this; it would cost her and my father dearly to pay for it.

Montego Bay was a special place, even then. The international airport had been completed in 1947 and Pan American Airways was beginning to lure beach holidayers from the U.S. with ads proclaiming, "It is January on the calendar but June in Jamaica," and telling Americans that Montego Bay was "a winter haven for the pleasure-loving international smart set." It already had something of that reputation with the British and North American political and economic elite who had their winter residences in the area — most notably Lord Beaverbrook with his eighty-acre Cromarty estate that was visited by the likes of Prime Minister Winston Churchill, Noel Coward, Ian Fleming, Grace Kelly, and Errol Flynn.

For the people who actually lived there, of course, all this was on the periphery. My grandmother lived in a small house on Dome Street. She had worked in the Panama Canal Zone at some point and she had a white china gravy boat stamped at the bottom as belonging to the U.S. Army mess. I suspect she worked there as a cook, because she was an excellent cook. Her beef soup was especially delicious, and she sold it locally from a small cook shack on Church Lane.

She also made a wonderful cornmeal porridge with coconut milk and cinnamon leaf, sweet potatoes and cornmeal pudding on the coal stove, and an amazingly good stewed catfish. My mother inherited her love of cooking and I must admit that, in my own way, I have as well.

Cornwall College, which then had only 200 students, was about a ten minute walk from my grandmother's house. The school had a reputation for both academic excellence and, in the British boys school tradition, a focus on transforming boys into men through sports. Though, as mentioned, I was more drawn to the latter, the academic side turned out to be important to me: Cornwall was one of the first schools in the West Indies that offered real science courses, including courses in chemistry and physics.

But this school, too, was steeped in the British imperial tradition with school uniforms and head boys and a very stern motto: *Disce aut discede* (learn or leave). And of course, once again, we learned British history and the British perspective on everything, and a large number of our teachers were British expats. I think this heavy imperial baggage helped guide me toward the sciences, which were less weighted by unrelenting Britishness than the humanities courses.

Still, I found the academics easy, to the point where most subjects held little challenge for me. The teachers must have realized this because a short time after my arrival I was moved up a grade, which at least forced me to take the classes more seriously.

But I was happiest on the field, the pitch, and the track. Those endless days playing cricket and soccer in the back yard had been good training, and I found that I measured up well against my compatriots on the sports fields of Cornwall. Intramural sports were highly organized and vigorously contested, and I also played on school teams. So, I was able to quickly make a name for myself at the school.

I learned that you got a lot of leeway at Cornwall if you excelled at sports. I broke the high school record for the cross-country mile race and was selected for the All-Schools Soccer Team (the actual games were not played that year because of a polio outbreak on the Island); the possibility of a pro career was real, and I thought about getting a university track scholarship. Cornwall was so sports friendly that I was even excused from classes to practise or travel to cricket matches when I was playing for my parish team.

Everyone was obsessed with sports in Montego Bay, and it seemed the whole city was there to watch Cornwall College win the national soccer championship for the first time in thirteen years. I was fortunate to score the winning goal in that game on a free kick. During that season, I was known for scoring a goal in every game — even though I played defence. In some Montego Bay restaurants, I could go in and eat and the bill would be waived. That is how local athletes were treated. On this intense diet of sports, with the privileges they offered me, I was able to coast through high school to matriculation.

Looking back, I cannot really say that this sporting life was wasted time. You can learn a lot from sports. You learn those clichéd but no-less-valuable life lessons of giving it your all, being a team player, and never quitting. You also learn about sportsmanship. The good and the bad.

I was playing in the men's soccer league at the Montego

Bay Guild Club when one of their big forwards, Vivian Collymore, found himself all alone in front of the goal and launched a bullet of a shot that hit our goalkeeper, point-blank, on the shoulder. There was a loud crack of breaking bone as the ball deflected right back to Collymore, with our goalkeeper now writhing on the grass. But Collymore did not shoot the ball into the open net; he let it pass him by. Instead, he went to help the injured opponent. That always impressed me. Even among opponents, there is a duty to protect each other.

But of course in sports you also have examples of the other sort of behaviour. I once was given a lift by an opponent's father to a game twenty kilometres away. When we soundly beat his son's team, he simply abandoned me there, drove off without telling me. In any conflict or competitive situation, I came to understand, it is better to leave any animosity on the field of battle and move on.

Sports also allowed me, after graduation, to see a little more of the world. A tour was organized to play soccer, softball, and cricket with teams in Cuba. The cricket games were played against members of the then-large Jamaican expat community working on the Cuban sugar cane estates, but the soccer and softball matches were with the local Cubans.

A group of twenty-eight of us flew to Guantanamo Bay in a small, noisy, propeller-driven plane that bounced like a bucking horse on the air currents. It was my first time in an airplane, and my fear was offset by the thrill of being in the sky and by the spectacular view of the sea and coastlines. After we landed at Guantanamo Bay and passed through customs, we were taken to our hotel, where that night we were formally welcomed by the mayor at a banquet held in our honour. After a week at Guantanamo Bay, we spent a few days in Camagüey and then a few more in Santiago.

I found it interesting to compare Jamaica and Cuba. In some areas, Jamaica seemed more advanced. In others, it looked like Cubans were more advanced. For example, the poverty on the plantations in pre-revolutionary Cuba was crushing, worse than I had seen in my country, but on the other hand, Cuba seemed to have a more advanced transportation system. Still, most Cubans looked at us as more privileged, and I remember one very poor woman actually asking me if I would marry her daughter, presumably to get her out of their abject poverty. However, the hospitality was, as anyone who has ever been to Cuba knows, incredibly warm, to the point where our play sometimes deteriorated under the weight of it. As one of my teammates, Constantine "Conny" Campbell, put it, we "won the first game at each venue but then lost the other games. Perhaps . . . because the hosts entertained us by partying each night."

Conny also learned the hard way that pre-revolutionary Cuba could also be a risky place. On our first night there, he was pickpocketed while we were at a late-night club. When David Cooke and I, another player and friend of Conny's, heard about it, we kicked in to give him a new stake. Conny and I became lifelong friends after this incident, and eventually we would leave Jamaica for Canada together.

Conny Campbell and me, 60 years after our arrival in Canada.

By the time of the Cuban excursion, I had already started work at the West Indies Sugar Company (WISCO), Frome Estate, the large sugar plantation in our region. I already knew a few Cornwall graduates who were working there, including Conny. He was a year older than me and had started working at WISCO the year before. I had been given an introduction to the job by my uncle, who also worked there, but I think what confirmed my decision to take the job was the fact that WISCO also had a highly developed sports program with a competitive league made up of teams from its dozen or so operations on the Island. With a Cornwall College graduation, I could work there in some clerking capacity, live on site, and earn some money while also playing for the company's soccer team. I took the job with high hopes.

CHAPTER THREE

COMPANY CLERK
AT THE SUGAR ESTATE

When I arrived at the Frome Estate gate in 1953, I was eighteen years old, and what struck me was the enormity of the operation. Frome occupied 30,000 acres, stretching from Shrewsbury to Little London and completely engulfing the towns of Frome and Grange Hill. The estate was made up of five sections (Shrewsbury, Frome, Belle Isle, Mint, and Masemure), each subdivided into three or four farms. There was also a central compound, Frome Central, where the administrative offices, the factory, the residences of senior staff, and the social club house were located. Each section had a section manager, an overseer, a section clerk, an assistant section clerk, and a stores clerk, and each farm had a timekeeper and scale clerk.

Along with my awe at the size of the place, I was excited at the prospect of living on my own for the first time and having money in my pocket. This was my first big adventure outside the protection of school and family.

On that first day, I went to the hostel where the clerks were housed. It was a long building not far from the main gate, with a verandah along its length. The rooms came off the verandah and at the end was a common kitchen and dining area. Some of the Cornwall boys who were already working there in some clerking capacity told me that they had all pitched in to hire a maid who cleaned the rooms, took care of our laundry and cooked the meals. My roommate was Neville Miller, whose father was the vice-principal at Cornwall and who, for some reason, had the nickname "Maestro." My friends told me it was hard work at Frome during the harvest, but it was not a bad life.

My job was at the scale house in front of the main gate. The scale clerk's job was to weigh the trucks carrying sugar cane from the farmers who sold their crops to Frome. The company had vast fields of its own but the new plant's twenty-four-hour production was so prodigious that it also purchased all of the cane from small surrounding farms.

Inside the gates, a hoist lifted the sugar cane off the trucks and loaded it on a railway car that took it into the factory where the sugar juice was crushed out and then put through a dehydration centrifuge to yield pure sugar.

The weigh scale job turned out to be an exhausting one because of the schedule, which accelerated as harvest approached. It began at twelve hours a day and the days lengthened when farmers pleaded with us to weigh their loads in the middle of the night as they sold off their stored cane. During the height of the harvest, our shifts were increased to sixteen hours a day, and we went flat-out seven days a week. The job became one of pure endurance; my life was divided into two parts work and one part sleep, with no time for anything else.

Frome is a name that all Jamaicans know. It was one of the largest sugar producers of the sixteen estates that made up West Indies Sugar Company, and in 1938 it was the site of the bloody labour dispute that in many ways was the crucible in which modern Jamaica was formed.

At the centre of things were, as always during this period, Alexander Bustamante and Norman Manley. On April 20, Busta gave a barnburner of a speech in Kingston, denouncing governor Brandis Denham and his legislative council and stating his support of the workers at the Frome Estates, who were demanding a $1-a-day wage. This added fuel to a growing fire. By the end of April, the situation at Frome had reached a crisis point.

On May 3, the *Gleaner* reported: "The old factory on the estate, which up to Friday had been grinding cane, is entirely in the hands of the strikers . . . I hear police shooting, followed by shrieks and cries . . . I can see men on the ground. Some are motionless, others are staggering to and fro or crawling away on their hands and knees. The strike has culminated in stark tragedy. A few minutes later I hear that three are dead, eleven wounded and that the police are making many arrests."

Four people were killed that day at Frome, three by police gunshots and one by a police bayonet. On May 4, the *Gleaner* reported that "the known cases of persons suffering from wounds has not exceeded twenty-five, the arrests up to yesterday afternoon reached ninety-six."

The events at Frome sparked strikes and demonstrations across the Island. The government ordered the arrest of strike leaders Alexander Bustamante and his assistant, William Grant, charging both men with sedition. The street battles continued the following day with two more people killed in clashes with government forces.

Fearing that the whole Island was about to break into open revolt, my namesake, governor Brandis Denham, declared a state of emergency on May 25. But this only increased the anger on the streets. On May 30, to try to calm things down, he released Alexander Bustamante from jail and hurriedly appointed a commission to enquire into the disorders.

But the stress was too much for the governor. The next day, May 31, he had his fatal heart attack at Government House. He was replaced by Charles Campbell Woolley as acting governor of British Jamaica. In the following week, six more protesters were killed by police. On June 14, Campbell Woolley announced that a royal commission would immediately be sent from Britain to investigate the conditions that had led to the uprising. Bustamante and Norman Manley were given assurances that the workers' demands would be addressed by the government.

This was one of the last times that Bustamante and Manley would work together. In 1938, Manley founded the

People's National Party and Bustamante formed his own trade union, the Bustamante Industrial Trade Union, and then in 1943 established the Jamaica Labour Party.

For its part, the Frome Estates simply carried on supplying the British imperial market. It was just too lucrative a business to give up. In the almost 300 years that the British had controlled Jamaica, estates like Frome had returned enormous profits — the first 175 years from slave labour, the last century or so with minuscule wages while sugar profits built many Downton Abbey–style mansions and great estates not only in Jamaica but in the United Kingdom. The company went ahead with construction of the new Central Sugar Factory, the most modern in the Caribbean at the time, and the first central factory to be established on the Island. By the time I arrived there in 1953, all was quiet and the struggles seemed like ancient history.

As the harvest drew to a close, my work schedule began to ease. We returned to six-day weeks, with Sunday off, and the post-harvest WISCO sporting season began with regularly scheduled cricket games and soccer matches between us and the nineteen other Jamaican sugar factories. This meant time off for practice and travel to some of the games, which were very much part of the company culture. We played to win and there was no doubt that your standing in the field was reflected in your standing at the job.

During this slow period I was moved into an office job as a payroll clerk, filling in the employment record slips with taxes and other charges itemized for the year for each

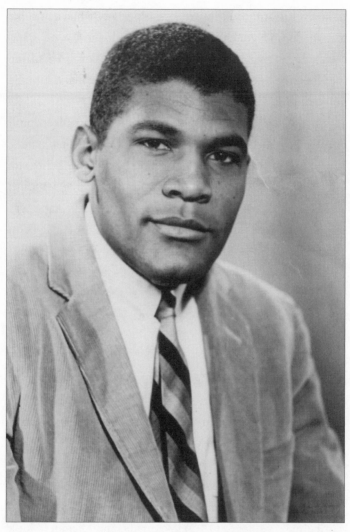

Me, starting out as a WISCO clerk in 1953.

employee. We had to balance these against the payroll for each farm — and there were several farms within the estate. We used those old cranking adding machines and it could be an excruciatingly slow process, especially when a mistake was made and you had to hunt through the list of 1,200 numbers looking for the error. From this you learned the art of slipping a few cents in here and there to make sure the numbers balanced in the end.

Payday was on Friday, and the people in my office would take the payday cash out to the farms to pay the field hands. With Sunday off, we spent Saturday night visiting the bars in Savanna-la-Mar, the bustling seaport ten kilometres south of Frome, from which much of the Frome estate sugar was shipped. Compared to the company town atmosphere in Frome, Savanna-la-Mar offered a welcome sense of the real world. It was especially exciting for us — we were, after all, still only teenagers. We were drawn to that raw energy that lights up Caribbean ports on a Saturday night.

Although I was enjoying life on the estate during this period, I was also looking ahead. I had no concrete plan, but I knew that I did not want to spend my life as a clerk. And my mother had convinced us that the surest way out of a stagnant situation was education. During my first year there, I learned that some of the management people, like the estate research manager, had gotten degrees at the Ontario Agricultural College (OAC) in Canada, and I began to look into it. To be accepted into a two-year diploma program, all you needed was the equivalent of Grade 11 education and agricultural experience, which I had from working at Frome. If you did well in the first year of the diploma program, you could switch into the four-year degree program.

What made the OAC so attractive compared to similar colleges in the British Commonwealth was the price. The tuition for Commonwealth students at the school in Guelph, Ontario, was $100 a year, and room and board was $300 a year. In comparison, the tuition at the Imperial College of Tropical Agriculture in Trinidad was a way-out-of-reach $4,000 a year.

I sent away for the OAC application. With the low tuition and boarding costs, I believed I could make enough money working during the summer holidays to pay my way as I went.

I also liked the idea that it was a foreign college. I wanted to see the world and I was beginning to find Jamaica frustrating in its colonial mentality. One incident that came to symbolize this was something that happened to Conny.

He had suddenly come up against the complex colour hierarchy that was in place at Frome. The managers tended to either be expatriate whites from Britain or "fair skin" Jamaicans; they lived in large houses with beautiful grounds. In fact, the upper managers' houses in the main compound were built on the very edge of the company golf course, which was immaculately kept by special groundskeepers. The head office staff lived in much more modest lodgings and were mostly mixed race or, as Conny put it, people with "milk in their coffee." The clerks and the field workers were almost all Black Jamaicans.

In one of life's ironies, and perhaps a sign of the changing times, several decades later I would visit the mansion of the estate manager when my brother-in-law was promoted to that position. Inside, it was as luxurious as I imagined and

I was most impressed by the colonial setup, which included a buzzer installed under the dining room table to call in the servants from the kitchen when the diners were ready for the next course or wished to have the table cleared.

At the time, the colonial racial differences seemed to be most intensely noted by the mixed race people, whose aspiring glances were always turned toward the whites at the head of the table. But despite the racial hierarchy among the Frome staff, there were no colour restrictions as far as being a member of the staff club, which had first-class facilities such as tennis courts, and I was sometimes, often to my surprise, invited to play tennis with the wives of some of the managers, and indoor games like billiards with the managers themselves.

The incident with Conny began over a billiards game. He was part of the company tournament, and he had a game scheduled with one of the upper-class English managers, Mr. Quayle. When Conny arrived at the billiard room, Mr. Quayle wasn't there. He waited, but Mr. Quayle didn't show up.

The next day Conny received a call from Gladstone, one of the organizers of the tournament, who wanted to know the results of the game. Conny told him that Mr. Quayle was a no-show. Then he added, "If Mr. Quayle wants to play me, he knows where to find me."

I was listening to the call. Knowing what kind of bootlickers staffed the head office, I suggested to Conny that he call Gladstone back to tell him not to use his exact words, since they might be interpreted as disrespectful toward Mr. Quayle.

Conny reached for the phone to call, but Mr. McIntyre, the office manager for the central office, was already on the line asking what on earth had gotten into Conny, using such an insulting tone in his message for Mr. Quayle. There was a second call from a "high colour" (light-skinned) Jamaican, Mr. Hayle, who summoned Conny to his office and asked if he had gone mad. Conny realized in that instant that all of the upward mobility that he had been dreaming of "was coming to a screeching halt," as he put it. The irony was that while the office staff was having fits of outrage at Conny's "impertinence in the face of his superior," when Quayle himself finally saw Conny, he immediately apologized for not making it to the match or remembering to phone to cancel. Mr. Quayle understood the obvious — it was he who was in the wrong, not Conny — and he had the decency to be embarrassed by the fact.

The incident was enough to make Conny decide to quit Frome and join me in my Canadian adventure. He admits that at the time and for years after, he dreamed of returning to Frome to get revenge on those who had so bitterly attacked him over his offhand message to Mr. Quayle. But he didn't return, simply because he couldn't find a job in his field in Jamaica or even an opening at the university. Instead he made his life as a celebrated soil scientist in Canada, winning numerous scientific awards and an Order of Canada. It was definitely Canada's gain, and Canadians can thank the small-minded colonials in the Frome Estate for this addition to their country.

While we were preparing to leave Jamaica for the Ontario Agricultural College, colonial Jamaica was busy taking its last gasp by preparing to celebrate the 300th anniversary of the arrival of the British, who drove the Spanish from the Island in 1655. This much hyped tricentennial celebration seemed odd to most Jamaicans — after all, the British came as slave owners — but I mention it here to give another sense of the mentality of those in power in Jamaica at the time.

Part of the celebration was a national beauty contest that tried to balance some of the racial divisions in the country with a papered-over unity. The beauty contest, called *Ten Types — One People*, gave awards for different complexions. These were the official categories:

Miss Ebony, black women
Miss Mahogany, women of cocoa-brown complexion
Miss Satinwood, women of coffee-and-milk complexion
Miss Allspice, part-Indian women
Miss Sandalwood, pure Indian women
Miss Golden Apple, women of peaches-and-cream complexion
Miss Jasmine, women of part-Chinese parentage
Miss Pomegranate, white-Mediterranean women
Miss Lotus, pure Chinese women
Miss Apple Blossom, women of European parentage

This colour shade–obsessed contest obviously revealed much more about Jamaican society's real divisions than its supposed unity, regardless of how the British framed it.

The newly crowned Queen Elizabeth did not visit Jamaica for the tricentennial. Instead, she sent her sister, Princess Margaret. During the five-day visit, the Princess did the royal job of inspecting troops, accepting bouquets, going to the horse races, wearing odd-looking hats, and waving at crowds. The main press and popular interest in the Princess, however, focused on the celebrity scandal of the day: whether or not she would marry her boyfriend, the divorced captain Peter Townsend.

By the mid-1950s, Jamaica — while still firmly in the colonial grip — was gradually moving toward independence with popular elections in which Manley's People's National Party and Bustamante's Labour Party vied for control of the legislative assembly. There was even a dream of a greater West Indies with a federation of the West Indies, which was formed in 1958 and brought together ten British Caribbean colonies into a single country, like British North America before 1867. It was a hopeful idea but, as it turned out, a short-lived one.

But these were not my dreams. Mine lay further afield. In Canada. I had just turned twenty years old that year, and by the end of August my suitcase was packed and I was prepared to make the leap into the unknown world of a country that was a complete mystery to me.

CHAPTER FOUR

ONTARIO AGRICULTURAL COLLEGE
AND VIOLET'S REFUGE

In those days, all flights from Jamaica to North America passed through Miami. Although small by comparison to today's airports, Miami seemed large and chaotic to us. Conny and I were supposed to have a two-hour wait for our flight through New York to Toronto, but when we arrived at the departure gate we learned that a major storm was sweeping across northeastern North America and our flight would be delayed not for an hour or two, but up to twenty-four hours. We headed into the airport restaurant that looked out over the tarmac and watched the endless stream of planes landing and taking off. We were, for a time, oblivious to our surroundings, until we noticed that others who had arrived after us were being served — their orders were being taken and their meals were being brought and some of them had even had time to finish and leave. We had still not even received menus from the waiter. We tried to flag him down, but he continually managed to overlook us or to look through us without seeing. We then realized we were being refused service. The thought infuriated me.

The next time the waiter passed nearby, I stood up so he could not miss seeing me. I honestly don't remember what I said, but Conny says that I used a string of profanities to express how objectionable I found their behaviour.

At the time, I did not know what risk I was taking, but looking back I can see that this incident could have turned out very badly for us. Blacks who stood up and made demands in the American South in the 1950s were not treated gently. Broken bones and a jail cell, or worse, were a real possibility. But perhaps because it was an airport, a transitional point, and we were clearly not American Blacks but "foreigners," the waiter and the manager reacted by trying to calm us and assuring us that we would be served if I would just sit down and be quiet. I did. They served us and we ate our lunch with a kind of sullen pleasure.

This was our welcome to North America. Conny and I had a long time to contemplate the incident while we spent the night in the airport waiting for our New York flight. We wondered what we could expect ahead in Canada. From our history, we knew only that Canada and Jamaica were both products — or, maybe more correctly, byproducts — of the same empire that pushed and pulled, and in many cases forcefully and brutally dragged waves of humanity around the earth to serve its political and economic interests.

On our island, which the Indigenous peoples called *Xaymaca*, the first inhabitants were displaced, killed outright, or driven into the hills, and Africans were brought in for forced labour with whites installed as overlords. It is the story of the Americas wherever the land and climate allowed plantation or estate farming. Our emancipation was won long ago, but the order of things was set when slavery ended. The people who had been enslaved and brutalized for more than a century received no imperial compensation; instead, the exploiters and brutalizers were compensated for their loss of free labour.

Canada was early on designated as a white country. Indigenous peoples were pushed onto tiny reserves in a system that was later admired and imitated by the South African Boers. French Canada was populated first by church- and court-dominated colonists, English Canada by retired army officers, the underclass of the poor of London and Liverpool, the landless Scots, and the starving Irish. Then, when more bodies were needed to fill the vast prairies and provide a market for the railway men, hundreds of thousands more of the landless were brought in from Eastern Europe.

Yet the British Empire gave Jamaica and Canada a common bond. For much of this early period, the two colonies were even linked with Britain in the three-corner trade, with British manufacturers travelling to Canada, where codfish were loaded for Jamaica to feed the workers, and from Jamaica the wealth of our tropical produce was shipped to Britain. This trade became an important outlet for early Canadian capital, and it is no coincidence that the Bank of Nova Scotia opened a branch in Montego Bay before it opened a branch in Toronto.

But we had heard from others who had gone to the agricultural college ahead of us that, despite the Commonwealth bond, Blacks really weren't welcome in Canada. It did not have the restrictions and overt racism of the American South or the up-front whites-only policy of Australia, but it was not known as a friendly place for us.

What Canada specialized in, I was to learn, was a kind of underhanded racism which was very much in effect in the 1950s and in historical terms was as Canadian as maple syrup. The exception, of course, was that period in the mid-nineteenth century when the Underground Railroad gave freedom to an estimated 30,000 American Blacks. There was another brief bright spot in the 1850s when the protectorate of British Columbia was actually run by a Black man, James Douglas, a Hudson's Bay employee living in Victoria. Bucking the trend, Douglas brought in Black settlers from California and even today you can find a Black graveyard on Salt Spring Island. Before and after these shining moments, early Black immigration was discouraged, sometimes fiercely.

From the 1890s onward, when Canada was aggressively searching for new immigrants from around the world, Canadian immigration worked to exclude Blacks from entering the country. The man charged with enforcing this unofficial policy for most of the first quarter of the twentieth century was W. D. Scott, who was appointed superintendent in the department of immigration in 1898 and remained in that post into the 1920s, controlling access to Canada on a day-to-day basis.

Canada was offering free land in the West and advertising around the world to try to entice settlers into the country. Among those who saw a welcome opportunity to start a new life were American Blacks who, like many other Americans, sent requests to Ottawa for immigration applications. This soon presented a dilemma for the immigration officers, who were rushing to approve the entry of more than one million immigrants. Panic went through the department, and W. D. Scott demanded that his officers find a way to screen out Blacks. He insisted, though, that these exclusion policies be administered from behind the scenes. What they settled on was a procedure whereby, when they received an application from an American of uncertain race, the Canadian immigration officer would discreetly send a letter to the applicant's local U.S. post office asking if the person was Black or white. Many of the postmasters' replies identified Blacks with the most odious racial slurs, and these letters can still be found in Canada's immigration archives.

The Black applicants were then left endlessly waiting — ignored, like Conny and me at the Miami airport restaurant. The effectiveness of this under-the-table racism can be seen in the numbers. Of the 1.3 million people admitted to Canada in the first decade of the last century, only 900, or less than one tenth of one percent, were Black. Canada explained this discrepancy by suggesting that Blacks were not suited to the Canadian climate. Even the *Chicago Daily News* scoffed at this ridiculous response by pointing out that a Black man "had been Perry's sole companion when he reached the North Pole."

But Canada and W. D. Scott would never admit that they were enforcing this invisible colour bar. On July 29, 1914, W. D. Scott, still superintendent of immigration, wrote to his agent at Halifax, W. L. Barnstead:

> Sir: I notice in a number of Board cases the cause of rejection includes the statement that the person rejected is a Negro and that instructions have been received to prevent the entry of Negroes in every possible way. While it is true that we are not seeking the immigration of coloured people . . . I do not think it is advisable to insert any notice of the instructions or policy of the Department in a Board decision or other correspondence beyond stating in the proper place that the person is a Negro. I am sure you will appreciate the view I have expressed and will understand the reason therefor.

That is, finally, how the Canadian system would work. Do whatever you can to keep Blacks out of Canada, but don't leave a paper trail. "None is too many." That famous statement on Jewish immigrants fleeing Nazi persecution in Europe would also apply to Blacks in Canada. And like anti-Semitism of the period, it would only be spoken of in backrooms in whispers.

To receive our temporary student visas, Conny and I had to sign a paper promising not to stay in Canada under any circumstances after the student visa expired. In fact, we were told that even requesting permanent residency in Canada would result in our immediate deportation.

By the time we arrived in Toronto, it was the end of the afternoon on the day after we had left home. We took a cab to Union Station downtown and caught a train to Guelph, seventy-five kilometres west of Toronto.

The Ontario Agricultural College (OAC) had been founded in 1874, and it was a mix of Victorian architecture and squat new post-war buildings. We were installed in Johnston Hall, the great limestone building with an imposing clock tower overlooking the school's expansive front lawn. We saw students below, young men and women — the school also had home economics degrees for women, and a veterinary college — drifting toward the dining hall.

Conny and I joined the line and we were encouraged, amid this sea of white faces, to find other Blacks and even a few Asians from Commonwealth countries. In fact, of the 1,000 students enrolled, 100 were from British West Indies and most of those were from Jamaica. There were even four or five others who, like Conny and me, had worked at WISCO.

Part of the reason for the strong Jamaican presence was the activities of the deputy director of agriculture in colonial Jamaica, C.D. Hutchings, a white West Indian from Turks and Caicos who had attended the Ontario Agricultural College in the 1930s and was still very active in the alumni association. He was working to improve Jamaican agriculture, and he promoted the school within Jamaica and wrote about Jamaican agriculture in the *OAC Review and Alumni News*. I would later learn that the OAC, with its ten percent Black population, was about as integrated as Canada got at the time.

But what I remember most strongly from those first weeks was my introduction to Canadian food. My first meal seemed, like almost all of the meals I ate at the OAC, to be built exclusively around the potato, for which Canadians seemed to have an inexplicable passion. I had rarely eaten them in Jamaica, but in Canada, I learned, the potato in all its forms — baked, boiled, mashed, fried, and scalloped — was king. And the only spice Canadians seemed to have discovered to go with potatoes was salt. I ate them, of course, but I longed for my grandmother's cooking and even the well prepared and spiced food we had at Frome.

That first night, I fell into bed after supper, exhausted from the twenty-four-hour trip and a bit stunned by the unfamiliar surroundings. But a few hours later, in the middle of the night, we were woken up by older classmates banging on the door. We could hear muffled laughter and it was a few moments before we realized that we were targeted for frosh week. We were hustled down the hall with other freshmen on our floor and out into the cool night air. I remember the surreal feeling. By this time Conny and I had gone with almost no sleep for two full days. We were marched under the football field bleachers with the others and ordered to quack like ducks. This was our initiation into the school and there was no choice. We quacked.

I don't remember any resentment at all about this. This is how things were at universities in those days, and everyone accepted it in the light spirit in which it was intended. What I mostly remember from that night, and the succeeding nights when we were hustled outside into the darkness for some kind of foolery, was being exhausted.

Still, that first week allowed me to get an initial measure of my classmates and a sense of my own position there. This was my first experience at being what Canadians now call "a visible minority," and I discovered that, in general, on an individual basis, most of my fellow students were decent people. Some would become close friends. But even with that rather special atmosphere at the OAC, there were glimpses of some of the issues that would have to be faced in the world beyond the campus. In the college paper, advertisements showed Black people with bones in their hair shaking spears around a fire cooking a pith-helmeted "explorer" under the lines: *What makes the Zulu live in trees / and Congo natives dress in leaves* . . . This type of portrayal was considered completely normal by my classmates.

There was also at least one chaplain at the college in Guelph who counselled girls not to go out with Black students. One incident still stings sixty years later: when one of the students butted out a cigarette on the floor, another said, "Oh, don't worry, we'll get some nigger to clean it up."

At the time, though, it would be difficult to find a Canadian who would admit that racism was an issue here. While the college chaplain was quietly telling the girls to stay away from the Black students, the student association was sending letters to the U.S. protesting its racist policies.

Dresden, a town in Southwestern Ontario, was in the grip of a battle to win service for Blacks in local restaurants. I will sum it up briefly because it gives a snapshot of race relations in Canada at the time.

A small farming community, Dresden was known as one of the terminus points of the Underground Railway and as the home of Josiah Henson, whose life story was the inspiration for the novel *Uncle Tom's Cabin*. But in the 1950s, Blacks in the region, who were fairly numerous because of the Underground Railway, were routinely refused service at the local restaurants and lunch counters. Hugh Burnett, a local carpenter and Black World War II veteran, had had enough. When he was refused service at Morley McKay's lunch counter in Dresden, he founded the National Unity Association (NUA) with other local Blacks to press their case. They went first to the local authorities. They collected 115 names on a petition to end discrimination and took it to the Dresden mayor asking for a referendum on the question: "Do you approve of the council passing a bylaw licensing restaurants in Dresden and restraining the owner or owners from refusing service regardless of race, colour, or creed?"

The result was devastating for the NUA members. Only 108 residents voted that restaurant owners should serve everyone, and 517 voted against. The racists were in a clear majority.

But Burnett did not give up. He went to Toronto to get the support of the Joint Labour Committee on Human Rights, an organization that included Donna Hill, the mother of author Lawrence Hill and singer Dan Hill, and Bromley Armstrong, the then-twenty-six-year-old Jamaican-born labour activist who would later become a close friend of mine.

Delegations met with Ontario Premier Leslie Frost and succeeded in having him pass two acts to outlaw discrimination in the province: the Fair Employment Practices Act (outlawing workplace discrimination) and the Fair Accommodation Practices Act (making discrimination illegal in restaurants, stores, and other public-access areas).

Despite these laws, people in Dresden continued to practise discrimination, and, in 1954, the NUA staged sit-ins at Morley McKay's restaurant, which was flouting the provincial anti-discrimination laws. The court challenge that resulted ended in victory for the NUA, bringing a legal end to overt discrimination in the province. Despite the victory, Burnett was forced to leave town after his daughter's life was threatened and citizens boycotted his carpentry business. He was living in London, Ontario, when the first Black patrons were finally served in the Dresden restaurant.

This was the situation in Southern Ontario while I was at the school. The attitude of the Morley McKays of the world would continue to flourish underground in Canada for some time, and even today it raises its head more often than most would care to admit.

But during those first few weeks at the OAC I was immersed in the day-to-day. After frosh week, I was able to sleep through the nights, but the days remained full of obstacles to be crossed or climbed over, as is the case for any young person trying to acclimatize to a new school and a new life in a new country.

The course work itself was challenging, a mixture of both pure and applied sciences, although I found my Cornwall education had left me well prepared with the basics. My schoolmates, many of them Canadian farm boys who had been sent by their families to acquire modern skills that they would then bring back to the family farm, were mostly unpretentious and, in their own way, quite open to the world, at least in comparison to their small-town Southern Ontario cousins in Dresden. The presence of the home economics and the veterinary colleges gave a little more variety to the campus — but, as mentioned, the women had been warned not to associate with Black students.

Both Conny and I worked hard. We were determined to get the marks we would need to enter four-year degree programs; my plan was to attend two years of college in Truro, Nova Scotia, and two more at McGill University's Macdonald College in Montreal. We both buckled down and worked toward our goal, and my only real extracurricular activity was playing on the school soccer team, which helped remind me of the pleasures of home. That was cut short, however, by the arrival of the cold. Early in the fall I got my first charley horse from playing with cold muscles, and very soon after that the season ended. Winter was upon us.

Your first Canadian winter, as any Caribbean person who's lived through one can attest, is astonishing. I watched in disbelief as the temperature fell to below freezing and then kept falling, plummeting to $-20°C$ with the snow piled up into four-foot banks on the roadways. Canadian winter was, I learned, something to be endured — but at the same time, in that first year, it was something almost too extraordinary to be believed. From the warmth of the dorm room, you couldn't help but be affected by the beauty of the wind-driven snow across the schoolyard, the clean sweep, the sparkle. There was the thrill of newness in it that I must admit has pretty well worn off sixty winters later.

The days were also much shorter. And in those long nights of my first Canadian winter, I often found myself missing home, missing, along with family, the usual things Jamaicans miss: the food, the warm Caribbean sun, and the easy social graces that I find in most Jamaicans.

In the end, both Conny and I survived the winter. We did well in our first-year courses — I was happy to find myself in the top five of my class — and we were both accepted into the four-year degree program. But Conny would be staying at Guelph to complete his studies — largely because of a quirk of Cornwall College's recording of math scores that convinced the registrar he was some kind of math genius. For some reason, Cornwall gave marks in math up to 150 rather than a 100. Conny was actually so-so in that subject, earning 100 out of 150, but the registrar mistook it for a perfect mark and enrolled Conny in the four-year course at Guelph. Today Conny is a highly respected Canadian scientist, and he tells this story of his mistaken math prowess with great pleasure.

Both of us were happy to discover that the school ended its year early so that its young farmers could go home for planting season. Classes did not start up again until after harvest, giving us four months off. After the last day, I headed into Toronto to look for a job that could earn me enough money for my second year at school. Other Jamaicans had given me the address of a rooming house on Manning Avenue, near Queen Street, run by a Jamaican woman named Violet Williams (later Blackman, when she married a Barbadian railway engineer.)

Violet's house would be my real home away from home for many years. I would come back to it each summer when I was a student, and I visited often for years afterward. It was Violet who gave me the first glimpse of a Canada I could make my own: that small world of Black Canada that I discovered was peopled by some of the most remarkable men and women I have ever met — quite a number of them expat Jamaicans.

The house itself was a simple square red-brick two-storey with a narrow porch pushed right up to the sidewalk. It was only a half a block from Queen Street in a neighbourhood that was already alive with multi-ethnic energy from postwar immigration — Italian and Portuguese groceries, and a mix of discount shoe stores, laundromats, and cafés. Groups of Eastern Europeans were still moving in, stragglers from the war, and they would soon be joined by waves of Hungarians fleeing Europe after their unsuccessful 1956 uprising. The neighbourhood was like the reverse of the butterfly effect: a big upheaval somewhere in the world would eventually make small but real changes in the makeup and the rhythm of life on Toronto's Queen Street.

Violet was at the centre of things. She was born on May 22, 1900, in White River, a village just outside of Ocho Rios, Jamaica, 150 kilometres up the coast from Industry

Cove. She immigrated to Canada in 1920 as a nanny, which was one of the few ways a Black person could enter Canada in the first half of the twentieth century. She approached each of her employers in her typical down-to-earth manner: "The first thing I would tell them is that I would give them the respect they were due, and that I expected the same in return." She saw her work as a means to an end, a business, not subservience, and never gave up her independence; at all times, she maintained her own residence.

She became a community leader in 1924 when Marcus Garvey visited Toronto to set up a branch of his Universal Negro Improvement Association (UNIA). Violet joined the movement and eventually worked her way up to female president. The Toronto chapter grew in importance in the 1930s when the U.S. banned Garvey from entry, and he held his annual UNIA conventions in Toronto in 1936, 1937, and 1938. During the 1937 conference, he conducted a summer school in African philosophy in Toronto, and visited Nova Scotia and New Brunswick. His influence in Canada was enormous.

His torch was still burning bright when I arrived in Toronto in spring of 1956, sixteen years after his death; UNIA and Garvey's philosophy were still thriving in the city, and very much so at Violet's house on Manning Avenue. As mentioned, it was at Violet's kitchen table where I had my first real initiation into the Black struggle in North America. She and her band of activists lived it every day.

Violet became like a mother to me, and soon I was referring to her, only half-jokingly, as *Mom*. She not only helped me establish myself in the city, including directing me to employment, but she would waive my rental payment when I was between jobs, and she would even slip me a few dollars in pocket money when I was broke. We remained close friends until her death at the age of 90, and I was honoured when I learned that she had requested I give the eulogy at her funeral. I remember saying then that Violet could be as calm and peaceful as the chalk-bottomed crystal-clear White River that flowed through her village and she had a great sense of humour and an incredibly lively intellect, but when necessary she could be "as determined and turbulent as an angry Caribbean Sea." She was in every way a force of nature and an inspiration to the generations of men and women she took in, protected, and mentored.

As soon as I was settled in and told Violet that I was looking for a summer job to earn enough money to return to school, she sent me to see another legendary figure in Black Toronto, Harry Gairey, also a fellow Jamaican. For twenty years, he had been a railway porter and one of Toronto's leading Black activists.

I met him at his office in the bowels of Union Station. I remember that he seemed from the first meeting like a no-nonsense guy, someone who was used to getting things done. I told him that I had come from Jamaica the year before to study at the agricultural college in Guelph, and I needed a summer job.

He nodded. "There's a job loading freights." He told me the name of the foreman I should see. And that was that.

At the time, I was just a kid looking for a job. But in later years, I would get to know Harry Gairey as the partner to Violet in the Garvey movement. At some point, they had a romantic relationship and Harry fathered one of Violet's two daughters, but when I met them, I don't believe they were romantically linked — they were in their fifties and were more comrades in arms.

Gairey was born in 1902 in Runaway Bay, a town only thirty kilometres away from Violet's village of White River. What brought them together in Toronto was political struggle — both were passionate adherents of Marcus Garvey, whose own birthplace, Saint Ann's Bay, was almost exactly halfway between Violet's White River and Gairey's Runaway Bay.

Harry Gairey's family had left Jamaica and moved to Cuba in 1907, when he was only five years old. While still a child, he worked in a sugar mill and then a cigar factory. He came to Canada with some friends in 1917, taking a ship to New York City and continuing on to Niagara Falls, where he crossed into Canada. He must have hit the right border guard: he was a teenager, with no papers, who said he just wanted to see Canada — they waved him through. After arriving in Toronto, he rented a room in the home of a Jamaican couple who treated him like a member of the family. There were very few Blacks in the city. Gairey remembered that you could walk up and down Yonge Street for days and run into only a railway porter heading to work, or some domestic workers shopping on their day off, but it was a rare thing.

After several years in Toronto in the 1920s, Harry guessed that he got to know virtually every Black person in the city and they would often socialize together. Blacks, he said, often lived in the same neighbourhoods as the Jewish immigrants "because at that time the Jews were treated like the Blacks. You'd see a Jewish man driving a little cart with a horse and picking up old clothes, garbage, newspapers, and that sort of thing. So they weren't very well thought of ..."

Gairey had begun working with the Canadian Pacific Railway in 1936 as a sleeping-car porter, and he helped organize the Brotherhood of Sleeping Car Porters, which obtained changes within the CPR that would allow for Black persons to be treated and promoted fairly. It was a time when, for some reason, train workers were expected to be Black and CP would even send him across the border to New York state to recruit new porters because there were not enough Blacks in Canada.

Gairey first gained notoriety throughout the city in 1945, when he took his fight against Jim Crow at the local skating rink to the media and to city hall. This incident gives a good sketch of the man and the times.

It was just after the war and Gairey was working on the Toronto–Ottawa train. On a Saturday afternoon, his son Harry Jr. and his school friend, a Jewish kid named Donny Jubas, were hanging around the house, and Harry Jr. asked his father for some money so they could go to Icelandia, the skating rink on Bathurst Street. Harry was on his way out the door to work, but he remembered reading in the paper that the Icelandia discriminated against Jews. So he told his son, "If they discriminate against Jews, you haven't got a chance, my boy."

His son said not to worry, they would behave themselves. Harry said, "Be careful." He gave them some money and headed off to the train station.

When Harry returned on Sunday night, his wife waited until after supper to tell him their son had, in fact, been refused admission to Icelandia.

She told him that Donny had been ahead of him in the line and said, "Two tickets."

The ticket seller glanced at Harry Jr. "We can't sell your friend a ticket," he said. "We don't sell tickets to Negroes."

The two boys left together.

Any Black parent can understand how Harry Sr. felt about this. Even though he'd anticipated the refusal, he was heartbroken and enraged. He stewed in bitter thoughts all night. On Monday morning, he headed directly to the College Street office of Joe Salsberg, then alderman for Ward 5.

Salsberg's office was on the second floor, and Harry bounded up the stairs and told him the whole story, knowing, he later explained, "that the Jews will fight — because I needed help to get this thing straightened out."

He was right about that. Salsberg said, "Mr. Gairey, meet me at the city hall on Tuesday morning at the council chambers on the second floor."

As soon as he arrived, Salsberg introduced Gairey to the mayor, Bob Saunders, and the whole council and said, "Mr. Gairey, tell your story."

Gairey, himself a veteran, said, "It would be all right if the powers that be refused my son admission to the Icelandia — I would accept it — if when the next war comes, you're going to say, 'Harry Gairey, you're Black, you stay here, don't go to war.' But, Your Worship and gentlemen of the council, it's not going to be that way. You're going to say he's a Canadian and you'll conscript him. And if so, I would like my son to have everything that a Canadian citizen is entitled to, providing he's worthy of it. Thank you, gentlemen of the council."

At a time when virtually all of the men in the room were veterans, Gairey's words struck a chord, as he knew they would. The story was on the front pages of all of the city papers the next day, and students from the University of Toronto picketed Icelandia, demanding an end to racial discrimination.

In the ensuing weeks, the story turned up in papers in Europe and the U.S., and Toronto City Council hurriedly passed an ordinance that businesses must not discriminate because of race, creed, colour, or religion. Today his victory is recognized in Toronto in the form of the city-owned skating rink called the Harry Gairey Ice Rink on Bathurst Street, not far from where the Icelandia once stood.

After my meeting with Harry, I was hired to load freight cars at the CP yard at Union Station. For a young guy with an athletic past, the work slinging boxes wasn't difficult, and during lunch breaks I would head up to the great station hall to watch the passengers coming and going. I would do this with another OAC student, Ray Scrowpad, who was in the veterinary course. I had only run into him once at the school, when we were both heading back to the residence from the downtown pub. We started to hang out at the railyards and became good friends. His parents owned a motel on Lake Shore Boulevard, and I visited his home many times. A few years later, Ray would be important in helping me get back into the country.

After each shift, I was welcomed home at Violet's like a son, and I knew I was one of many young people this woman had taken care of. Her influence on young people of varying backgrounds produced chartered accountants, doctors, geologists, university professors, editors and publishers, nurses, a priest, basketball professionals, successful businessmen, and an airline pilot. Indeed, I remember 12 Manning Avenue as a home, a cultural centre, and a spiritual refuge.

Through the UNIA, Violet even managed to give us a social life. She had taken great pride when, as women's head of the UNIA, she had led the drive for the purchase of the UNIA community centre at 355 College Street, which became a monument to Black progress, a place the community could call its own, and a rallying point. Twice a week, the centre held gatherings and dances for young people, students, and young women working as domestics, providing a much-needed place for young Toronto Blacks to meet. Violet ran these events herself, sometimes bringing in Black soul music bands from Detroit.

She was also the security for the events. In the hall, the chair that Marcus Garvey had sat in during his many visits to Toronto was given a prominent place and Lord help the hapless person who tried to sit in it. Violet would give them a no-nonsense dressing down. (Even though the College Street UNIA building was sold just before Violet's death in 1990, the chair still has a respected place in the offices of the Jamaican Canadian Community Centre in the Jane-Finch area.) If you were causing real trouble at one of Violet's socials, she would tell you to get out or, if you were Jamaican, she would threaten to tell your parents. Everyone listened to her, she had that kind of forceful personality that you didn't even think of defying.

Even with all that, UNIA was not her only activity. To help people financially, she worked to found the Toronto United Negro Credit Union and served as its first vice-president. She also worked with Gairey in organizing the Negro Citizenship Association, which lobbied for changes in Canada's immigration laws.

In putting together my notes and researching the period, I came across a letter Violet wrote to the citizenship association in 1955, apologizing that she was too busy to attend the Tuesday meetings because she was running the UNIA dances. Still, she enclosed a $40.00 donation, an enormous sum in those days, along with her $2.00 yearly membership fee, and encouraged "each and every one of you who is able to do something for the cause, not to wait until you are asked, but just feel that it is our responsibility and duty, one and all, to go ahead and do something so that we may build up our treasury in order that the Officers may have something to work with." Her commitment to helping people, to making the world a better place, was total. She remains an example to us all.

The strength she instilled in us allowed us to cope with the real challenges that were also part of Canada in the 1950s and have persisted into the present time. My encounter with the police on Parliament Street in my late seventies was only one of many such instances. The first one happened in my first year in Canada. One evening as I was walking home, a car slowed beside me and a man in civilian clothes demanded that I come over to him. I ignored him and kept walking. The car suddenly accelerated and drove onto the curb in front of me. Two men leapt out and one flashed his badge. "We're police officers," he said. "We want to talk to you."

I told him, "Sorry, I didn't know you were police . . . I almost took off running."

The policeman smirked and patted his gun in the shoulder holster. "You wouldn't have gotten very far," he said.

After a few questions they let me go, but my heart was pounding as I turned the corner. I knew, from the look in his eyes as he spoke, that the police officer was not bluffing. Despite the individual kindness I experienced from some Canadians, I understood that this could also be a dangerous world for a young Black man. And the worst was still ahead: Canadian racial resentments would increase exponentially with the increase in Black immigration. I would have to navigate it with great care.

My summer in Toronto was ending and my life was about to undergo another leap into an unknown: a year of study in Truro. Nova Scotia, I understood, was far to the east of Toronto, and I knew it only as a place where Jamaican Maroons had been exiled by the British in another century and that most had found it so inhospitable that they left, at the first chance, in a boat heading to Africa. My hope was that things had improved in Nova Scotia since then.

CHAPTER FIVE

NOVA SCOTIA BLUES
AND MONTREAL DELIGHTS

To get to Nova Scotia at the end of the summer, I climbed into a boxcar in the railway yard in Toronto. It was Harry Gairey's idea. When I told him that I was going to begin the first year of my degree course in Truro, he told me to ask the guys which boxcars were scheduled for the through-trip to Nova Scotia. I boarded with a duffle bag, a big lunch, and a Thermos of water for what turned out to be a twenty-four-hour trip. The train left in the early afternoon and rattled down the rail through Kingston, Montreal, and Quebec City, with several hours spent in dark and noisy train yards. But for the most part we seemed to be just passing through the endless Canadian forest. For the cool night, I used my winter coat as a blanket and my duffle as a pillow and slept a deep and largely uninterrupted sleep in the swaying-back-and-forth and clickety-click of the rails.

I arrived in Truro in late morning. There was no residence at the school at the time — although one was under construction — but the school had given me a list of local boarding houses when I applied. When I showed the address to the station master, I was told it was not far. I shouldered my duffle and walked.

Even though the sun was shining on that early September day, I was not filled with hope. I could see that Truro was a far cry from Toronto, or even Guelph. It was a small farming town and a railway junction of the CN and CP lines, and you could see from the peeling paint and the chipped and cracked concrete of the sidewalks, and from the collection of modest businesses and clapboard houses, that this was not a wealthy place. It seemed like a town that had already passed its prime — but that even in its prime had never amounted to much.

I was greeted at the door of the boarding house by a middle-aged woman. As she showed me around, she told me her family had been farmers with land outside of town but had moved into Truro a few years ago. Her son, Archie, was going to the college, and two other students, another Jamaican and a Guyanese, were also boarding at the house. So I understood why I was given this address. This house accepted Black students.

The woman seemed nice, but I knew this place would be far from the busy residence at Guelph or the high energy of Violet's rooming house in Toronto. When I learned that the woman expected me to share a bed with the Guyanese student, I told her no, I absolutely would not, and she hurriedly made other arrangements, bringing another bed into the room. But it was an indication of what lay ahead for me in Truro. Nothing would quite work. I would be in exile there.

Nova Scotia itself had a lousy reputation among Black people. In fact, most of the Blacks who arrived in the first couple of waves of immigration had quickly decided against staying and headed off, literally and figuratively, to sunnier climes.

The first to arrive were the Black Loyalists who came at the end of the American War of Independence. British authorities in the American colonies had promised freedom to enslaved Blacks who escaped and made their way into British lines. Large numbers arrived and many took up arms alongside the British, as did a number of Black freemen, in a regiment called the Black Pioneers. Approximately three thousand of these Black Loyalists sailed to Nova Scotia in 1783, travelling on both navy and chartered ships.

Unfortunately, they were met with broken promises. The land plots that they were given were a fraction of the size of those given to the white Loyalists and they were located on unproductive lands, generally in the middle of nowhere. The result was the creation of Black towns that had more in common with townships in South Africa than colonial settlements.

The fact that they were not welcome in the colony had been made brutally clear in 1782 when the early arrivers in

Birchtown were attacked by white soldiers who resented Blacks getting work that the soldiers thought they should have. The Birchtown white soldiers' riot is today credited with being the first race riot in North America.

In the aftermath, many of these War of Independence refugees drifted away. Ten years later, 1,192 African American men, women, and children gave up and left Nova Scotia and sailed to Freetown, Sierra Leone, where they set up their own community, leaving a smaller population behind.

The next wave of Black emigration was from Jamaica, and most of the Jamaicans lasted a shorter time than the Black Loyalists had. On June 26, 1796, over 500 men, women, and children — Jamaican Maroons — were deported to Nova Scotia after a failed uprising against the British. Small farm lots, again in the least fertile areas, were provided to the Maroons, who immediately complained of being harassed by Christian missionaries trying to convert them. The local governor reported that, after suffering through the harsh winter of 1796–97, the Maroons expressed a desire to be given arms and "sent to a climate like that they left, where they may take possession with a strong hand." On August 6, 1800, the Maroons departed Halifax for Sierra Leone, arriving on October 1 at Freetown.

The next major migration of Blacks into Nova Scotia occurred between 1813 and 1815 with Black War of 1812 refugees settling in many parts of Nova Scotia, including Hammonds Plains, Beechville, Lucasville, and Africville.

Those who remained from these three migrations would make up the core of the Nova Scotia Black community. Their numbers would be bolstered by the arrivals during the 1800s of many others on the Underground Railroad. But they, too, would find a less-than-welcoming embrace in Nova Scotia.

The official desegregation of schools and most public institutions in Nova Scotia did not occur until 1954, and segregation unofficially persisted long after that. Even desegregated schools like the one in Truro had segregated washrooms when I arrived. Since the 1780s, the Black community in Truro had existed mostly in poverty and had been subject to the most blatant racism. Its prospects had not improved much since.

Although the agricultural school was completely integrated, I was confronted by the long-lingering unofficial segregation in the town when I tried to go to the Friday night social at the Anglican church. It had been our family church in Green Island, but in Truro I was stopped at the door.

"You can't come in here," I was told.

I looked around and saw I was the only Black in the line-up. The reason for the refusal was clear. I saw one of the department heads from the college standing nearby and caught his eye. He looked away. I was left standing there, furious at the department head, at Truro's racism, and above all at the church that was barring me. I can mark that point in my life as the moment when I definitively turned away from religion. How could anyone associate with an institution so riven with racism that it barred church members from a Friday social? This one act gave lie to all of the principles the church was supposed to stand for.

That incident was an early taste for me of what Black Nova Scotians had grown up with and continued to live with in the 1950s. Most were understandably beaten down by this. The Black area in Truro was across the river from downtown in the swampy lowland at the foot of the area called Bible Hill, where the Nova Scotia Agricultural College campus was located. Local Blacks were downtrodden to the point that most young people quit school at sixteen or earlier and went to look for an unskilled labourer job. When asked why they left, they would say that schooling was useless for them because, no matter how much education they had, they would just end up cleaning someone's house or working on the railway.

The situation was so dire in Nova Scotia that Marcus Garvey visited the province in 1937 to urge young Nova Scotian Blacks not to give up. A paraphrase from his speech in the Menelik Hall in Sydney — *emancipate yourselves from mental slavery; none but ourselves can free our minds* — would, four and a half decades later, make it into a Bob Marley song.

That is what we are often left with when confronted by white racism. We have to find a way to rise above it using our own means. In fact, the whole quote from Garvey's Sydney speech gives a good sense of what he was about and his relevance today: "We are going to emancipate ourselves from mental slavery," Garvey told the Nova Scotia Blacks, "because whilst others might free the body, none but ourselves can free the mind. Mind is your only ruler, sovereign. The man who is not able to develop and use his mind is bound to be the slave of the other man who uses his mind, because man is related to man under all circumstances for good or ill."

One Black family in Truro that had taken the Garvey message to heart was the Jones family, with ten children —

one of them my age — who I got to know fairly well.

The Joneses were known in the area for their grandfather, Jeremiah, who had been a war hero in WWI but had been refused the Distinguished Conduct Medal (DCM) he had been recommended for. The incident was recorded by his commanding officer. His company had been pinned down at Vimy Ridge by machine gun fire, and Jeremiah crawled to the machine gun nest under heavy fire and tossed a hand grenade into it, killing several soldiers, then took the rest of the German unit prisoner and marched them back to the Canadian lines. He was immediately recommended for the DCM, but resistance within the military to awarding a Black man the medal was formidable. It took ninety-three years of lobbying by his family before it was finally posthumously awarded in 2010.

By that time, Jeremiah's grandson, Burnley Allan "Rocky" Jones, had become an internationally recognized human rights and anti-poverty activist who would at one point be described as "Canada's Stokely Carmichael." I would often hear about him in the news later, but at the time, I knew only his family for their strength and pride among a people who had faced the grinding racism of rural Nova Scotia for more than a century.

The place of Blacks in Truro set the stage for my two largely unhappy years there. I missed not only my home in Jamaica but also my life in Toronto. For a young Black man, the segregated politics of the place was not only deeply offensive, but it also made life excruciatingly boring. There was simply nothing to do. The college didn't even have a soccer team, and I was finally driven to join the hockey team — despite the fact that I didn't skate. The school league let me keep my boots on and put me in goal. It was my first up-close examination of hockey, and I must admit I was surprised by the violence of it. I saw players swinging sticks over their heads like clubs or slashing with them like machetes. Recalling the gallantry I'd seen in other sports, as when Vivian Collymore rushed to the injured goaler instead of taking the rebound, I found hockey lacking. I did not become a big fan of the game — although I admit this with some reluctance, since I know in this country it really is more our national religion than a mere sport. And indirectly, decades later, it would finally make me a convert in an unexpected way.

With any real social life cut off from me, all I had was schoolwork. I spent most of my time in my room, buried in my books. The result was that I once again received very good marks — again in the top five in my class. But all the time I was there I was wishing I could escape back to Toronto. My life improved a little in the second year when I moved into a newly built residence. At least I was around more people my age, including girls from the nearby nursing school who were invited to Friday night dances. Equally important, living in residence meant that I didn't have to take those long, bitterly cold walks to the campus in the winter.

But as soon as classes ended in the late spring of my first year, I hitched a ride with a fellow student to Toronto, where I could live a much fuller life.

In Toronto, the post-war economic boom was still resonating. There were jobs everywhere. You only had to look at the board at the government employment offices and pick your job. I remember one employment counsellor suggested I go to work at the iron foundry because, as a Black man, I would not be bothered by the heat. But Canada's booming economy required workers so badly that the country could not afford to discriminate.

To build up funds for the next school year, I worked for CN during the evening and at the old Gooderham and Worts distillery on Mill Street during the day. The distillery job couldn't have been easier. It consisted of rotating the barrels according to a schedule that left time between rotations to take a nap, hidden away on the stacks.

My Toronto summers would feature a wide variety of jobs. I was fired from one of them for doing wheelies on the small tractor we used to haul the yard garbage and losing control and hitting a wall. But that wasn't a worry. If you lost a job, you simply went back to the employment office and came out with a new one. In this case, I found a new job at the Old Vienna brewery near University and Dundas Streets. My task was loading the soaker along the rolling tracks. When the empties came in, we would take them out and put them on a moving belt that took them to a huge vat where they were soaked and then cleaned. What stood out there was how many workers were half or fully drunk for most of the day, since we were given two beers at morning coffee break, two beers at lunch, and four more during the rest of the day. It was a job that could make an alcoholic out of anybody and many of my coworkers spent their days stumbling around in a beer haze, which no one seemed to mind.

The multitude of available jobs gave us a freedom that is hard to imagine today, and it helped give my generation a more carefree life. You had the feeling you could go anywhere and pick up a job to survive and move on when you wanted. I sometimes think this fact alone helped shape the coming decade, the 1960s, when young people felt the freedom to move around and explore. If things didn't work out, you could always pick up a labouring job for a few days or weeks and save a bit of money for the next adventure.

My main adventure was my education, and that required working as many jobs as possible and saving as much as possible in the summer. But of course, I also had time for fun in Toronto. When I was staying at Violet's, I was still going to the Tuesday and Friday night dances at the UNIA hall on College Street. I also hooked up with my friends from Guelph, many of whom were also in Toronto in the summer, and met students from Jamaica and other West Indies islands who were attending the University of Toronto, and I played on a very competitive West Indies cricket team in the Toronto league.

One important friendship I made during this period was with Bromley Armstrong, who has become something of a legend in the Toronto Black community. Bromley was born and grew up in Kingston, Jamaica. He came to Canada in 1947, when he was twenty-one years old, and got a job at the Massey Ferguson plant. He decided to try to better himself by taking a welder's course, but, when he told his supervisor about it, the supervisor told him he should get his money back because Massey had never hired a Black tradesman. Only labourers. The colour bar became obvious when, after completing his course, Bromley applied three times for a welder's job and each time they told him they had no record of his application. Finally, Bromley turned to the local United Auto Workers union. He met the president and asked for help. The union leader made him an offer. If Bromley would become active in the union, he would help him. Bromley kept his word, and a few years later he was working with the union in the campaign to desegregate Morley McKay's lunch counter in Dresden. From then on, he devoted much of his life to fighting racism in Canada, and in later years I had the pleasure of working alongside him many times.

I met Bromley at Violet's place, shortly after I arrived in Toronto. In another indication of how small a world Black Toronto was at the time, Violet's daughter Eloise was married to Bromley's brother, and they lived with Violet. Our first meeting was at a party at his mother's house that Eloise and his brother had invited me to. I experienced Bromley's well-known directness firsthand when he spotted me standing alone and came up to me not to say hello but to ask, point-blank, who I was and who had invited me. After that slightly awkward start, we saw each other often over the years, and we tended to turn to each other when we needed support for a cause.

My Truro exile ended in April 1958 when I completed my second year there, and, as soon as classes ended — I didn't wait for the graduation ceremony — I made a beeline out of town. After another summer in Toronto, I headed to the Island of Montreal for the last stage of my education.

I was in a hopeful mood once again. McGill's Macdonald Campus, as it is currently known, is in Sainte-Anne-de-Bellevue, on the western tip of the island, where a narrow channel and a set of locks connect the two riverine lakes — Lac St-Louis, which is part of the St. Lawrence Seaway, and Lac des Deux Montagnes, which opens to the Ottawa River to the northwest. Ste-Anne's is about fifteen kilometres from downtown Montreal, and at first glance it had the look of a resort town, with a busy main street of cafés and shops and a lively bar called Joe's Night Club. I was joined at McGill by a cousin of mine, Neville, and we found a simple apartment in the upper half of a small duplex on Adam Avenue, not far from the campus. I stayed there for the first year then moved into the residence for part of the second year.

The second thing I noticed about Sainte-Anne-de-Bellevue, after the beauty of the town, was the fact that the campus was right next to a teachers college which was full of bright young women. In fact, while the Macdonald College had 200 young men in agricultural sciences, the neighbouring teachers college had 1,000 students, almost all of them women. We young men were like kids in a candy store.

As part of McGill, Macdonald college also had first-rate sports teams, and I quickly joined the intercollegiate soccer squad. It was a pleasure to get onto the pitch again with a competitive team. In 1960, the second year I was there, we won the intercollegiate championship. I had kept in good physical shape with the labouring jobs in Toronto, and I won the overall track and field award for the school. After Truro, life was good again. I have kept in touch with a number of teammates from that period, including Martin Barnard from St. Kitts, who I sailed the Grenadines with in his yacht; Don Parchment, now a photographer in Miami; and Laurie Sharp, who became one of Jamaica's biggest coffee producers and visited me in my Toronto home some fifty years after our championship win.

In fact, life in Sainte-Anne-de-Bellevue was almost too good. The campus was alive with parties, dances, and late nights at Joe's nursing a beer with friends and girls from the college. I met some wonderful people there, like author Merrily Weisbord, then a student teacher; she and her filmmaker husband, Arnie, are dear friends who often stay with me when they are in Toronto. But the partying was taking a toll on my grades. I was barely passing. I pulled back and hit the books to bring my score up.

I spent my last winter and summer at Macdonald College living with a group of roommates in a cold water flat that backed onto the lock. The winter was an ordeal. The stove was hard to start, so for heat all we had was a two-winged toaster that we kept on all the time — that and a lot of blankets. We also soon learned that we had to keep the tap running at all times to keep the lines from freezing, although we were grateful to discover that when they did freeze, the local firemen would come over and send an electric current through the pipes to defrost them.

It was a hard winter financially. To get through my first year there I had borrowed $200 from the emergency fund administered by head of Student Services, a Mr. Puxseley, who told me that when I had paid it back, I could borrow another $200. I paid it back with my summer earnings but when I went into the office in the winter for a renewal of the loan, I was met by the college dean, Dr. Dion. Puxseley was no longer with the school. I explained the situation to Dr. Dion, that Mr. Puxseley had said I was eligible for a new loan since I had promptly paid back the original one. But even while I was speaking I could see that look in his eye: he saw me as something less than an equal. And I was right. He dismissed me with unsmiling sarcasm: "Well, maybe you should go and see Mr. Puxseley then." I took the loan forms he had handed me and tossed them in the waste bin on the way out.

I managed to squeak through without Dr. Dion's loan. Most students were in the same boat — low on funds. But, being students, we also managed to scrape together enough money now and then for a night on the town in Montreal, which had a justifiable reputation in those days as a kind of open city. Even for Blacks. In an odd way, Black Canadians had some protection in the 1950s because of our low numbers.

I remember those last few months in Sainte-Anne-de-Bellevue as a happy time. When spring came and the weather warmed, the town turned into a resort again. The back of our apartment looked out over the canal and Lac Saint-Louis, and we were just a few doors down the main street from Joe's Night Club. I was finishing up my degree and was able to relax and enjoy being a young man in that charming little town. In the mornings I would make a coffee and sit out back watching the boats moving through the locks, and in the evenings I would watch the sun set over the lake. The streets outside my door would fill with villagers and students heading to the lakeside bars and restaurants that gave the town its charm.

It was, in many ways, a good time to be young in the world. The 1960s were beginning and change was in the air. Nothing concrete, but the world seemed to be taking new shape with new hopes and some new fears. In the Caribbean, the young Cuban revolutionaries Fidel Castro and Che Guevara were in the news for their defiance of America, something unheard of in our region up until then. At the same time, a new force was rising in the U.S. as Senator John Kennedy began winning primary after primary on the way to the Democratic National Convention in July and then the presidency in November. All during that summer, the desegregation battle was heating up in the American South, and a great wave of decolonization was sweeping across Africa with a stunning array of countries — Cameroon, Senegal, Togo, Mali, Madagascar, Somalia, Benin, Niger, Burkina Faso, Côte d'Ivoire, Chad, Central African Republic, Gabon, Nigeria, Mauritania, and both Congolese republics — all winning their independence in 1960.

The Cold War was also part of this background when the Soviets shot down an American spy plane and captured the pilot and then, to add insult to injury, successfully launched two dogs — Belka and Strelka — forty mice, two rats, and a variety of plants into space and brought them back safely the next day as a precursor of their first manned flight.

Other important developments were in the works. The Vietnam war was just beginning and the Beatles were spending that final summer honing their craft at the Indra Club in Hamburg. Then, that spring, the U.S. Food and Drug Administration announced it was approving the world's first oral contraceptive pill. The 1960s were ready for takeoff.

My strong desire was to remain in Canada, to put my degree to use here and to make my life in the country where I had been living for the past five years. But it would not be so easy. As mentioned, I had been forced to sign an undertaking that I would not even try to gain permanent residency in Canada after my schooling was finished, and regular immigration check-ins were required throughout my stay in Canada. They were keeping close tabs on us like prisoners on parole. I'd discovered this the summer before, when I was in Toronto and forgot to go to immigration for the periodic check-in. Within days, two burly immigration officers with military brush cuts were knocking on the door demanding to know why I had not shown up. These people were certainly not going to let me overstay. At one point, I tried to convince a professor to sign a paper indicating that my schooling was not finished — that I had more courses to complete. But he refused.

When my exams were done I headed to Toronto, still hoping for a reprieve and to be allowed to stay in the country where, by then, all my friends were, where my life was. It was a difficult couple of months. I remember one dismal afternoon sitting in a coffeeshop with a couple of guys I had attended Guelph with who were listing all of the job interviews they had lined up.

It seemed completely unacceptable to me that at a time when tens of thousands of Europeans were still flooding

A legitimate McGill graduate.

into the country, many with little education or immediate prospects — and in a few celebrated cases at the time, German and Italian immigrants were arriving with TB and still being welcomed — I was being shown the door, even though I was a Commonwealth citizen. Salt in the wound was the fact that the Germans and Italians, just fifteen years earlier, had been the key Axis powers that Canada, Britain, and the Commonwealth had lost hundreds of thousands of men defeating. My uncle had returned from the war stone deaf from manning the guns. But now, even TB-infected Germans and Italians were way ahead of me in the immigration line.

By this time, of course, I understood how Canada worked. The reason Canada still had so few Blacks was that the colour bars were still up at the immigration department. The first small changes to Canada's race-biased immigration regulations would be made in a couple of years. But the exclusions wouldn't be fully lifted for more than a decade.

When I finally headed to the airport with my return ticket to Montego Bay, I did not feel like I was heading home; I felt that I was being deported — that I was being evicted from my home, Canada.

CHAPTER SIX
JAMAICAN EXILE

When I passed the immigration gate into the main part of the Montego Bay airport, I looked around for my brother Winston, who was supposed to pick me up.

He wasn't there. Then he was. Standing in front of me, smiling. I hadn't recognized him.

That is how long I had been away, long enough for him to grow from a boy of eleven into a young man of sixteen years old.

Nothing, it seemed, was how I remembered it. At the airport, a new flag flew beside the Union Jack: a blue background and four white undulating lines with a golden disk in the centre, depicting the sun on the dark blue waters of the Caribbean sea. It was the flag of the new West Indies Federation.

My brothers and sisters: Winston, Desmond, Hyacinth, Barbara, and me.

On the way home to Industry Cove, we didn't talk politics. Instead my brother caught me up on family news. There was a lot to cover in five years. My sister Hyacinth had completed her training as an R.N., and Barbara, who had a biology degree, was teaching at a high school in Kingston — in later life she would go on to become the first Black headmistress of the high school she had attended in Montego Bay. My brother Desmond was back at home trying to make a go of the family farm. Jamaica was trying to become more diversified in food production and had brought in all sorts of agricultural incentive programs. Desmond was growing sugar cane and he had also brought cattle and chicken farming to the family land. This experiment only lasted a couple of years. Desmond would end up going to university in Oregon and receiving his doctorate at UCLA. Winston would later travel to Toronto, where he would work for CN and Toronto Transit before he started his own business. Our mother was still looking after the world, now in an expanded role as the local justice of the peace, but our father was slowing down at eighty years old.

That first evening was a celebration of my return. We were all happy to see one another, and it felt great to be sitting at the family table and living room again.

But that feeling did not last. When I woke up in my childhood room the next morning, I was very aware I was not a child. I was a twenty-five-year-old with a science degree from McGill University but without any economic prospects and cut off from the friends I had made over the previous five years. This was not going to be an easy time. I had only one goal — to get back to Canada.

I suspect this was not easy for my parents, either. I didn't know what to do with myself, and they didn't know what to do with me. I began to look for a local job in a halfhearted way while I sent job applications to Canada trying to find something that would allow me to get a work permit to return. One of the places I applied was the Protestant School Board of Montreal for a science teaching job. In the meantime, I looked around for temporary teaching work in my region.

It took three months to find it. While I was waiting for responses to my applications, I poked around the house. I looked up a few childhood friends and renewed some acquaintances, but most of these old friends were busy with their own lives in circles where I was a stranger.

In January 1961, a job opened up in Lucea at Ruseas High School and I took it, but I was still planning to pick up and leave for Canada at the first opportunity. This attitude did not sit well with the school principal, an ardent nationalist who believed that educated young Jamaicans had a duty to stay home and build the country. I told him that maybe those who received government scholarships to study abroad had some obligation, but I had gone abroad on my own and worked hard to earn money to pay my own way, without any help from anyone. I didn't owe any debt to Jamaica.

One pleasant interlude was a visit from Ray Scrowpad, my Guelph friend and former CN coworker. Ray came to Montego Bay on a holiday, and we spent most of it together with me serving as his guide to the area. Ray was by then already a fully accredited veterinary doctor, employed at an animal hospital in New England. I told him that I was trying to find a way back to Toronto or Montreal, and he understood. "If I can help in any way," he said, "just let me know. I'll be glad to."

I was still pinning my hopes on my application to the Protestant School Board of Montreal, and my desire for the job increased while I was at Ruseas High School because I realized that I really did enjoy teaching. I had a good rapport with the students — I wasn't so much older than they were — and there was real satisfaction in watching restless young minds focus on and grasp the principles of basic science. Knowledge of how the world works changes and enriches how you see life, and I was happy to help younger people along that path.

I also had time to play cricket on a local team at Watson-Taylor Park. I took a special pleasure in playing in Lucea in the stadium by the sea. On my first outing, I made 140 runs without an out in a match against the public works department, and immediately after the match I was invited to play on the parish team in a game scheduled for the following Saturday. Alas, in my at bat I scored what is referred to as a "strokeless duck," a big zero, and watched my teammates radically reassess my cricket skills.

As it turned out, my days at Ruseas High School were already numbered. In mid-March, the school principal came to me after class and said that he had received a request from a Protestant school board in Canada for a reference. He told me point-blank that he would not give me one because Jamaica needed my skills.

I was astounded by his hubris, his unilateral decision to order my life to suit his politics. By that time we were approaching Easter break so I kept teaching for a couple of weeks, but when the break began I told him I would not be back. I would not work for someone who would sabotage me like that.

I remember leaving and feeling that mix of exhilaration and fear that you get at these bridge-burning moments. When I visited my family in Industry Cove, my uncertainty increased when I told my father. He forgot his own admonition not to work for someone else, and he urged me to go back immediately and try to withdraw my resignation. He was worried that I was again without a job.

By that time, so was I. It was April, and there was no chance that I would find a teaching job in my region or anywhere until at least the fall. I was also finding myself increasingly bored by the limited choices in Lucea and Industry Cove. I decided, finally, to head to Kingston.

At first, I stayed with friends near the centre of town; then I boarded with friends in Mona, a northern suburb of Kingston near the University. I landed a job as a nutrition researcher in the government health department studying the ackee, Jamaica's national fruit. The government was looking at export markets in the U.S., but the ackee seeds in the early stages are toxic and this was raising flags with the U.S. health department. We were working to isolate and then remove the toxins. The job was interesting, and it did get me out of the quiet and somewhat isolated life in Hanover parish, but the pay was quite low.

In the end, it turned out to be a good move. It was an especially interesting time to be in Kingston. In 1961–62, the mercurial Alexander Bustamante and the intellectual Norman Manley battled over the timing, the nature, and the leadership of Jamaica's move toward independence. Manley and his Jamaican National Party had won the previous two elections by wide margins with his support for the British West Indies Federation. But by 1960, Bustamante and his Jamaica Labour Party (JLP) were dogging the governing party over a growing list of grievances against the federation. Busta complained that the decision to place the capital of the federation hundreds of kilometres away in Port of Spain, Trinidad, meant that Jamaica was being ignored. He complained that the share of Jamaican seats in the federation parliament was smaller than its share of the total population. But what was most irksome, Busta said, was that waiting for the federation to be ready for independence was holding Jamaica back.

As opposition to the federation grew, Busta and his JLP

pushed for a referendum on the federation project, and Manley, believing he could win it, agreed. But when the vote was held in September 1961, Busta's "No" campaign won 54% of the vote. Jamaicans wanted out of the British West Indies Federation, and Manley had no choice but to begin Jamaica's secession and then make a request to London to grant Jamaica its independence.

I was living in Kingston by the time the referendum took place, and the city was energized by the political tides lifting it toward independence. Optimism was also in the air because of the economic growth fuelled by the bauxite industry, with a Canadian company, Alcan, and two American companies, Reynolds and Alcoa, operating mines in the interior. This new bauxite wealth had come out of nowhere. Exploration had been done during the Second World War, but the first shipment had only taken place in 1952. By 1957 Jamaica had become the leading bauxite producer in the world, providing almost a quarter of all the world's supply.

For me, as part of the young educated class, Kingston in 1961 was a bit of a moveable feast. I met up with several of the friends from Canada who had drifted or been sent back to Jamaica. The city was alive in a way that it never had been before. With the good financial times, new clubs were opening up. It was the beginning of the era of ska music, the precursor to reggae that combined elements of Caribbean mento and calypso with American jazz and rhythm and blues. It was wildly popular in Jamaica, and it even found a niche in Britain with the British mods. At the time, reggae music was still on the horizon. A seventeen-year-old Bob Marley was living in Trenchtown, not far from my home in Mona, and had just recorded his first four songs under the name of Bobby Martell. They had more of a ska sound — this was before the Rastafarian influence on his music. Rastafarians in Jamaica were still very much discriminated against. Considered eccentric health food nuts and hippy squatters, they were constantly harassed and evicted by the authorities.

So ska ruled the clubs, and at night it flowed out onto the city streets. We visited the clubs or gathered on someone's verandah, and on weekends we headed to one of the beach resorts. In financial terms, I was struggling to keep up to my better-off friends but somehow I managed.

Ironically, this youthful partying in Kingston would lead me back to Toronto by way of an Appleton Rum–loving Winnipegger named Thompson. He was the roommate of someone I knew from Toronto, and he was notable for riding a bicycle with a bottle of Appleton Rum strapped on the back. But he also worked at the Canadian High Commission. At some point in the din of a party, I told him about my university days in Canada and my wish to return to Toronto to live. He didn't seem particularly interested — and I didn't expect he would be. But then at the next verandah party, he appeared with a set of immigration papers for me to fill out. I took them home and filled them out and I gave them to him the next time I saw him at yet another house party. A couple of weeks later when we were out on the town, he waved me over and handed me my Canadian entry visa. I was astounded. I had it. The high-living Winnipegger had arranged my re-entry into Canada, and I didn't even have to set foot inside the Canadian High Commission.

What I lacked were the funds for a plane ticket back to Toronto. Money was tight. My salary was so small that I was already finding it impossible to keep up the payments on my second-hand Volkswagen Beetle. At one point I had to head off the repo men and bribe them into leaving it with me — and from then on I had to be sure to park it in inconspicuous places. A plane ticket to Toronto at the time was $200, and that was far more than I was able to save. Help came from Ray Scrowpad. I contacted him and asked if his offer to lend me money to get back to Canada still stood. He said sure and wired me the $200.

Things were moving fast. I booked my flight for the first week of August and drove home through the interior to the north coast at Saint Ann's Bay, Garvey's hometown, and west to Hanover Parish. I didn't know how long I would be away this time, although I expected it would be many years, and it was a sad leave-taking because my father was getting old and I was not sure if I would see him again. As it turned out, I would not. The following year, both he and my maternal grandmother, Dinah Richards, passed away.

Jamaica was also preparing to move on. The date for the independence was set for August 6. Earlier that year Bustamante had beaten Manley in the election, so he would have the honour of leading the country into independence. While I was preparing to leave, the capital was being lavishly decked out for the ceremony while, as we later learned, the British were frantically destroying incriminating documents and shipping out sensitive files. But I was not unhappy to be leaving for Toronto. I did not even think of delaying my trip to take in the independence celebration.

Even though I was returning into uncertainty — I had only a few dollars in my pocket and an offer to stay with some friends in their basement flat in Forest Hill until I got back on my feet — I was leaving without regrets. Heading to Toronto, I felt like someone returning home. My last act in Jamaica was to call the repo company from the airport and let them know where I had left the Volkswagen with the keys inside. A short time later I was in the air, flying on the first leg of the trip to Miami, seven years after my first trip there with Conny. I was going home.

A few days later, Jamaica became an independent country. Across the Island, when the clock struck midnight on August 5–6, the new national anthem was played and the Union Jack lowered from flagpoles and replaced by the new Jamaican flag, with its black and green background criss-crossed by gold bands. The main event was held in Kingston with Busta and Princess Margaret (who had finally dumped Captain Peter Townsend and married a London photographer in what would become another drunken, scandal-plagued Royal marriage) decked out in formal wear for the midnight ceremony. For all Jamaicans, it was an undeniable moment of pride; in Kingston, 20,000 people, many adorned in the colours of the new flag, cheered as the Union Jack descended the flagpole.

The event did not go unnoticed in Toronto. Unbeknownst to me, the leaders of the Jamaican community, including my friend Bromley Armstrong, gathered at the King Edward hotel on August 6 to mark the occasion, raising the new Jamaican flag and stumbling their way through the unfamiliar words of the new Jamaican national anthem.

The night resulted in the formation of the Jamaican Canadian Association, which was spearheaded by Bromley and would play an important role in the fight for Black rights in Canada and in my own life as I established myself and became a Canadian citizen. But on the sixth of August I was in the basement flat on Dewbourne Avenue in Forest Hill, listening to the big news on the radio — not of the independence of Jamaica, but of a Canadian Premiers' Conference that W. A. C. Bennett was hosting in Victoria. On the seventh, I would begin looking for my first non-student job in my adopted country. Thanks to Appleton Rum and my Winnipeg friend, I was now a permanent resident — my Canadian adventure had begun in earnest.

CHAPTER SEVEN

PUTTING DOWN CANADIAN ROOTS

Within weeks of my arrival in Toronto, I was working on the rooftops of Bloor Street apartment buildings with the city at my feet.

The post-war economic boom was continuing, and I had been quickly hired by the City of Toronto as an air pollution researcher. This was around the time that *Silent Spring* was published, the book that alerted the world to the creeping environmental disaster, but it was still a time when we, as a society, had the most rudimentary knowledge of the dangers of the poisons we were putting into our air. Chemical threats were unknown or ignored. People smoked in elevators, DDT was still seen as a miracle pesticide, and highly toxic lead was still considered an excellent lubricant to add to gasoline. The view of the natural world was summed up by the Massey Ferguson ads published in the agricultural college newspaper when I was a student in Guelph, showing a perfectly groomed farm field and freshly painted farm buildings under the triumphant headline: *Where nature fought . . . and lost!* That was the majority view of nature in those days — an eternal enemy that we must not only confront, but vanquish.

My project was to assess some of the collateral damage in our battles by measuring emissions from burning garbage in apartment-building incinerators. Part of the day, I worked in the office on Grand Avenue in Etobicoke with the manager's son, who turned out to be an irritating snitch. But fortunately, I spent most of my time out in the field. My partner and I had a series of buildings to visit, most around the St. George subway station. We would contact the managers ahead of time and tell them to hold on to the garbage until we got there. Then they would fire up the incinerator and begin the burn while we climbed onto the roof with our sensor equipment.

In early September, when I started on the rooftops, I took pleasure in looking over Toronto, which had a much different skyline than it does today. I looked down into the green parkland and the Victorian architecture of the University of Toronto and the legislative assembly buildings at Queen's Park. The tallest buildings in the distance were the Royal York Hotel and the 34-storey Bank of Commerce building, which was, until that year, the tallest building in the Commonwealth. Other than these two, there were no buildings tall enough to obscure the view of the great blue expanse of Lake Ontario.

But already by the end of September, we began to feel the cold winds coming down from the north; by early October, the rooftop belvederes were often whipped by icy rain. I began to get a sense of how incredibly unpleasant it would be on those rooftops in the coming winter months when arctic blizzard conditions were in effect.

It was around this time that I read in the *Globe and Mail* about a high school science teaching position opening in Sault Ste. Marie, Ontario. Without a clue where this place was, I sent my resumé. To my surprise I quickly received a call at work from the principal. I tried to be discreet, but the boss's son had a habit of listening in on his colleagues' calls from his own phone and reporting to his father. So I had to get through unpleasantness at the office while I followed up with the Sault Ste. Marie job.

The transition was not a long one, however. The new Bawating High School was desperate for a biology teacher. The woman who had begun the year had just announced that her husband was being transferred to a job in New England, and she would be leaving in two weeks. The Bawating principal was so impressed by the fact that I had "researcher," as well as "teacher," on my resumé that he offered to fly me up to Sault Ste. Marie, some 700 kilometres to the northwest, for the interview that weekend.

It was a whirlwind visit. I arrived in the early afternoon and the principal met me at the airport. He gave me a tour of the school — which was a very modern design, built by the same architect who had just completed Toronto's city hall — then he took me to his house for dinner. I confess I played the good colonial, with the excessive politeness my mother had drilled into us, to the point that I even stood every time his wife came into the room as she served the meal. By late evening, I was on the plane back to Toronto almost certain that I had the job. I was right. The contract came in the mail a few days later, and I hurriedly prepared to move to Sault Ste. Marie.

Even then, I knew that this job would be temporary. The "Soo," as the locals call it, was a fairly tough blue-collar town on a sharp bend in the St. Mary's River that links Lake Superior and Lake Huron and, a bit further down, Lake Michigan. The big employers were the Algoma Steel mill and the paper mills fed by the northern wilderness that arced above the town. The Soo job would get me off the rooftops in winter and give me the Canadian teaching experience that I hoped would help me get teaching work in Toronto the following year. Toronto was where my friends were and where I wanted to live.

But even in that year of exile, I would not be cutting myself off completely from the city. As soon as the teaching contract I arrived, I took it to a Chevy dealer on the Danforth and bought a car to get me back and forth between the Soo and Toronto. It was not just any car. It was the now-classic 1957 Chevy Bel Air hardtop convertible — this one yellow with white trim and white sidewall tires — gleaming in the centre of the second-hand lot. At a time when the word "cool" was just beginning to appear in the lexicon, it was without a doubt a very cool car. I had no money, but the dealer was happy to finance it on the basis of the signed teaching contract, and I drove away from the lot in that flashy Chevy and into a new chapter of my life in Canada.

It was a ten-hour drive to the Soo from Toronto, passing through what seemed like the endless forests of Northern Ontario, through a Canada of bush workers and mill workers at a time when *diversity* meant Italian or Swede or Finlander instead of pure British, and the Jim Crow that was in force in many places in the region was not for Blacks, of whom there were almost none, but for the Indigenous people, who made up a significant part of the population. I would encounter Indigenous people often in the Soo — I believe they were mainly Ojibwe, now known as Anishinaabe — but the divide between them and Canadian society seemed complete. On the streets of the town they seemed to be invisible, and if they tried to intrude into the white world, they would be roughly ejected. For me, it was another indication that the famous superficial "niceness" of Canadians hid a darker reality.

That road between the Soo and Toronto was one I would come to know well. During the eight months I lived in the Soo, I made the drive to Toronto virtually every weekend except for the Christmas holidays, when I stayed in the city full time. So I was really only halfway a Soo resident — although my stay there would have an important impact on my life.

When I arrived on that late October weekend, I checked in to the YMCA, where I expected to stay until I found a place after a couple of weeks of looking. But shortly after I arrived, I called someone whose name I had been given by a U of T friend as a good guy to contact in the Soo. The name was Jack Horsley. He had just gotten married, but as soon as I called he invited me over. He was one of the friendliest and most good-humoured people I've ever met. He broke out the scotch and, with his charming wife, we drank and talked about Toronto, the Soo, and the world at large until it was getting late and I finally stood up to leave. He asked me where I was staying, and when I told him the Y, he said, hell, why don't you just stay here — you can sleep on the couch. And that is where I stayed for a couple of weeks, at Jack's insistence, until I found a place.

My new home was a house-share with two other guys in a good part of town. They were okay, although to be honest I hardly got to know them. I was busy during the weeks and gone on the weekends. In Toronto, I usually stayed with my cousin Neville, with whom I had roomed at McGill. So I felt like I had two home-bases.

Teaching took up all of my free time in the Soo. The class was Grade 9 biology and I had to start from scratch, building the lesson plans as I went, which meant late nights piecing together the course material for the following day. Biology is a big subject, but the hope is that you can teach these very young minds, most of them about fourteen years old, the basics of cells and genes, how organisms consume and regulate energy, and the mechanics of evolution. Most of the kids, I found, were up to it: they wanted to learn, and they wanted to have fun. I tried to make sure they had a mix of both.

One of my own lessons in Sault Ste. Marie was that Northern Ontario winters came early and lasted forever. After the first −30°C morning, I also discovered that I had to buy a block heater for my car. But on Fridays, even though it was already getting dark by 4:00 p.m., I would head out on that ten-hour drive to Toronto. I was not always alone. Jack Horsley and his wife would often join me on these weekend adventures, sharing the gas and keeping me awake as we headed through those endless, empty, and often snow-covered highways.

Toronto was becoming more interesting all the time, with an ever-expanding West Indian, primarily Jamaican, community. In 1962, Canadian immigration policy began to emphasize education, skills, and job prospects and, at long last, de-emphasize race. Visiting Canadian immigration teams were replaced by a permanent immigration desk at the High Commission in Jamaica. Between 1960 and 1964, 2,662 Jamaicans gained admission to Canada; between 1965 and 1969, that number had almost quintupled to 13,439, with a similar increase from the other West Indies islands. One important change came in 1967 with the establishment of the immigration point system that assessed immigrants purely on their skills in relationship to Canada and Canadians. Previously, immigration officers had been given wide discretion, and many used it to express their own racial preferences; the removal of this barrier encouraged mass emigration from the West Indies and other Commonwealth countries, as well as immigration of thousands of Haitians into Quebec, and the complexion of the country began to change.

Once again, these changes did not come out of the blue. An important part of the reason for the opening to Blacks was the lobbying of Harry Gairey's United Negroes Association. In the mid-1950s, he and a group of activists, including Bromley Armstrong, went to Liberal immigration minister Walter Harris and demanded a meeting. Thirty-five of them crammed into his office to make a plea for immigration reform. Harris made a few moves in that direction, but it was finally the Progressive Conservative Minister, Ellen Fairclough, who followed up and expanded on Harris's initiatives. Fairclough was a very liberal Conservative and, along with removing the most obvious barriers to Black immigration, she would later help Lincoln Alexander start his political career in Hamilton to become, in 1968, Canada's first Black member of parliament.

By this time, Harry Gairey was retired from the railway and running the West Indian Federation Club, where the weekend dances would often include young Jamaican and other West Indian women who were working as domestics. That was still the best way for many of them to get into Canada — because there was a demand for their services from wealthy white women — and many women such as Violet Williams and, later, Jean Augustine used the "domestic worker" opening to get in the door. The West Indian Club also had a restaurant where you could get excellent Caribbean cooking on a menu that always included curried chicken and curried goat. With the flood of new arrivals and the opening of places like the West Indian Club, a new Toronto was slowly taking shape.

But that still happened beneath the white surface. We knew our acceptance in Canada was tenuous at best. We saw this during the early 1960s in Canada's icy reception for one of the greatest athletes in Canadian history, Harry Jerome. In the early 1960s, Jerome was burning up the international sprinting tracks. In 1960, when he was only twenty years old, he tied the world record in the 100-metre dash at 10.0 seconds. A year later, he again tied a world record, this time running the slightly shorter 100-yard dash in 9.3 seconds, becoming the first man to co-hold world records in the 100-metre and 100-yard sprints simultaneously. After a new record of 9.2 seconds was set in 1962, Jerome matched it later that year. In 1964 he set a new world indoor record of 6.0 seconds for the 60-yard dash, and in 1966 he again tied the 100-yard dash record, this time at 9.1 seconds, a record that stood until 1974. He was clearly the world's fastest man and a Canadian whose family had been in the country for generations. In fact, his grandfather, John Armstrong Howard, had been the first Black Canadian in the Olympics, appearing in the 1912 games.

You would have thought Canadians would be swelling in pride to see their soft-spoken and extremely articulate countryman setting the world on fire. But throughout his career, the press focused mainly on Jerome's losses. In the ugliest incident, they called him a quitter when he badly injured himself at the Commonwealth Games in 1962. For almost all Canadians, Canada was still a white country; any who were not white were not celebrated as Canadians. We were here, we were growing in numbers, but we were still seen as, at best, a foreign presence. I followed Jerome's career with interest and admired his advocacy for Blacks in Canada after his running days were over. I was also pleased in later years to be able to honour him in a way that Canada had always refused. But at the time, for me and thousands of other Blacks, Harry Jerome was a litmus test for the country's racial openness. And the country was clearly failing.

*Our son Michael; Carol; our daughter, Nicole; me; and our other son
Kevin at Nicole's McGill graduation ceremony. Little did Carol know
that we'd become a family when we first met in 1963.*

But in the winter of 1962–63, while Harry Jerome
was setting world records, I was still building my life in
Canada, and it was in the Soo that I met the woman, Carol
Casselman, who would become my wife and the mother of
our three children.

I met her in the spring of 1963 through a friend of hers
who I'd been out with a couple of times. Carol and I ended
up in the same crowd, and she lived just up the street from
me on Pine Avenue in a large house with her family. Both
her father and grandfather were doctors and she herself
was planning to go into nursing. We hit it off, but because
we were aware of the potential resistance to a Black-and-

white relationship, we kept our relationship unofficial to her family.

Even though I was becoming seriously involved with Carol, my time in the Soo was quickly running out. I had applied and was accepted for a science teaching position at Forest Hill Collegiate in Toronto and I would be heading to Toronto to get settled there after the classes ended in June. That meant Carol and I would, for some time, be in a long-distance relationship. But she was happy to visit Toronto on many weekends and would eventually arrange to complete her nursing training there so we could be together.

On a late June morning in 1963, I left Sault Ste. Marie alone, happy to be driving off under the blue Canadian skies with the knowledge that in the fall I would still be teaching, a job I very much liked, in a city I had developed a real affection for. At that moment, I knew that I was on the right road and that I was living the life I was meant to live.

CHAPTER EIGHT
TEACHING AND LEARNING

Teaching is a labour of love. You do not get rich teaching in Canada or anywhere. That I knew. But at my new posting in Forest Hill, I was surrounded by wealth. Just north of the downtown area, Forest Hill is one of Toronto's richest neighbourhoods. The average income was and remains more than two-and-a-half times greater than the Toronto average.

The original Forest Hill village began as a bastion of Toronto WASPs, but in the post-war era it quickly emerged as the destination for the upwardly mobile Jewish community, and today about forty percent of the population is Jewish. But whether WASP or Jewish, what it was known for was the sense of privilege that wealth brings. When the village was annexed to Toronto in 1967, there was a special clause in the deal that required the city to pick up Forest Hill trash at their door, instead of forcing the inhabitants to put it out on the curb like the rest of the city. It was more than twenty-five years later that Torontonians learned that this concession to Forest Hill was costing the city almost half a million dollars a year, and they put an end to the practice.

The Forest Hill I moved into in 1963 was still that genteel self-governing urban village. It even had its own school board with a relaxed set of rules. The majority of the students at the school were Jewish, and most lived the sheltered lives of the children of the wealthy. They went to synagogue on Saturdays and were sent away to expensive summer camps when the school year ended. A soft protective cocoon had been created around them and I remember many had trouble with even the simplest tasks like lighting a Bunsen burner, because at home the maids took care of everything. But what they did have in abundance was a bursting curiosity about the world. They also had a kind of solidarity at a time when there was an important alliance between Black and Jewish activists. Just like Harry Gairey knew he would find an ally in Joe Salsberg in his fight against discrimination at the skating rink, these young, sheltered, idealistic students understood that for most Toronto WASPs, Blacks and Jews were considered second-class citizens.

But these kids were far from shrinking violets. Many had famous parents — Wayne's and Shuster's kids went to Forest Hill Collegiate, as did David Lewis's son Stephen, who went on to great national and international accomplishment. As did many other Forest Hill alumni such as Larry Grossman, who was leader of the Progressive Conservative Party in the 1980s; Lorne Michaels, creator and producer of *Saturday*

Night Live; lawyer Mark Wainberg; comedian Mark Breslin; and jurist Arthur Gans, who stood up to Mike Harris in disallowing his sale of Ontario Hydro. The first wave of post-war baby boomers at Forest Hill were young people on the move. The first year I was there, every Grade 13 student except one went on to university — and the one exception was simply taking a year off to travel in Europe.

Fortunately for me, the curiosity that most of these students showed about the world extended to chemistry and physics, the courses I was teaching. These are obviously not easy subjects, especially at the beginning when you have to look at the world in a new way and explore a reality that we cannot see, described in abstractions like periodic tables, physical states, and physical properties, with invisible elements like electrons and atoms operating under the special laws of motion, electricity, and magnetism. A tall order for high school kids, but I had had some pretty good teachers at Cornwall and was able to draw on some of their inspiration to enliven the material.

The classes were a pleasure to teach. I liked the brightness of the students and their sense of humour, and I think they liked mine. We were together not only in class but afterward because I was the "sponsor" — the word the school used for coach — of the tennis, track, and swim clubs and, of all things, the curling club. We were part of the Toronto intercollegiate system, but sports were not a big priority at Forest Hill. We were one of the few schools in Toronto that didn't have a hockey team.

In my years there, I developed real friendships with the kids. I was renting a place in Forest Hill, and they soon discovered where I lived. They would stop by for a visit, and the more daring would ask me to give them a ride in my '57 Chevy, which I was happy to do. In exchange, students would offer to wash it. I suspect that none of this would be allowed now — too many cases of authority-figure abuse have made us suspicious of this kind of intergenerational friendship — but that was a more innocent time and the world was fuelled, for good and sometimes for ill, by trust.

What I ran up against quite quickly, however, were the financial limitations that were part of the teaching life. Teachers were paid only ten months a year, with the last cheque coming at the end of June and then nothing until September. You were expected to save that portion of your salary to tide you over through the summer months, but virtually no one was able to do this on the already thin pay packets we received. Like university students, we had to find summer jobs. During the first couple of summers, I worked as a driving instructor and as a door-to-door Fuller Brush man, a job that attracted anyone with a gift of gab who was scrambling for money — but I soon found out this was not a gift I had, and I ended up with a closet full of Fuller Brush products.

This was not how I wanted to spend my summers, or my life. While I was trying to make it through to the September paycheque, I was also looking around for more lasting business opportunities — specifically to purchase, under favourable terms, real estate that I could rent out for a small additional income.

This became even more of an issue when Carol moved to Toronto to complete her nursing degree at Western

Hospital at Bathurst and Dundas and we made plans for a life together. Marriage plans were difficult, since mixed-raced relationships of any kind were still fiercely opposed in many quarters. We were not intimidated by the conventions of the day, but we knew that an ordinary wedding with dozens of friends and family members present would not be possible for us. We were married on July 7, 1965, in a civil ceremony with just my cousin Neville and a close friend of Carol's as witnesses. We drove down to Kingston, Ontario, for a honeymoon weekend. When we came back, we moved into a one-bedroom apartment at Keele and Eglinton.

Our relationship had been kept secret from her family and, at first, so was the marriage. I don't know their initial reaction when she broke the news to them over the phone; but after they had a short time to digest the fact, they invited us to visit them back in Sault Ste. Marie.

To say that I was unsettled at the thought of being introduced to Carol's family as her new husband is an under-statement. On the way up, I could imagine many scenarios on how the weekend would go and few of them were positive. All I really knew about them was that her father was a doctor and her mother was a nurse who grew up in New York City — an American, and that wasn't reassuring.

My fears melted away within minutes of my arrival. They welcomed me warmly and I never received anything but kindness from the family. I learned that one thing my father-in-law was relieved about had nothing to do with my colour, but my nationality. He was happy to learn I was Jamaican — and therefore a Commonwealth citizen — and not American. He had been overseas as a doctor with the

Canadian Army during the war and, like a surprising number of Canadians overseas, had developed an abiding dislike for Americans. In his case, it seemed to have something to do with some brutal instances of friendly fire from the U.S. forces. When Carol's sister married an American he was very disappointed in her. During weekends at their cottage on Lake Superior, he would react to the storm clouds coming across the lake from the American side by complaining about the damn fascist weather coming up from the south.

While I was still teaching, I found a property to buy in a ten-room rooming house on Huron Street at Dupont, close to the University of Toronto campus and handy for renting to students. There was a very nice fully equipped apartment upstairs in the house, but I couldn't afford to live in it at the time. I had to rent it out to a group of new arrivals to Toronto, American draft dodgers, with jobs at the university. They were part of a new wave of young counterculture types that were also having an impact on the city as Yorkville, the neighbourhood just northeast of the university, began to take shape in its 1960s incarnation. Living in a rooming house next door to mine was an Alberta girl called Joni Anderson, soon to become Joni Mitchell, who was making a name for herself at the Penny Farthing, a folk club on Yorkville Avenue at Hazelton.

I would like to say I passed my nights at the Penny Farthing Club listening to Joni hone her craft in the smoky haze of the coffee house, but during these years I had no time for anything. To make the rooming house work financially, I had to be my own maid service and janitor, spending nights and weekends doing laundry, cleaning the kitchen, and doing necessary repairs — and the often impossible job of collecting the monthly rent from my generally cash-strapped tenants. As someone who very often scrambled to make rent in my student years and who had been chased around Kingston, Jamaica, by repo men after my car, I tried to be a patient landlord. My sense of fairness was generally returned by tenants who, I believe, did their best to pay what they owed.

The 1960s were swirling around us. The Vietnam war was raging in the jungles of Southeast Asia, and the anti-war movement was spilling onto the streets of American and then Canadian cities. At the same time, Black America was in revolt. For several years, the U.S. had been following a politics of assassination with Jack and Bobby Kennedy, Medgar Evers, Malcolm X, and Martin Luther King all cut down in their prime. Especially after the murder of Dr. King, Black anger boiled over into riots in the streets with the famous "Burn, Baby, Burn" riots and the rise of ghetto self-defence forces like the Black Panthers.

In Canada, the race issue was first perceived as a kind of American echo, probably best summed up by the story told by Burnley Allan "Rocky" Jones about his sudden rise to prominence. While living in Toronto in 1965, he came across a demonstration in front of the U.S. Consulate.

"I noticed all these white people carrying signs and organizing a sleep-in. When I asked them what they were talking about, they said that Black people in Alabama didn't have the right to vote and were being beaten by police." Rocky went home and then returned with his wife to join the demonstration, as the only Black person. "Before I knew it, microphones were being pushed in my face, and the media was asking for my opinion. So, I said: 'Black people deserve to vote, and the FBI has to use its powers of arrest in Selma (Alabama).' The next day's headlines referred to me as Canada's Stokely Carmichael, and I didn't even know who he was."

Jones went back to Nova Scotia and founded the Halifax-based Black United Front (BUF), a Black nationalist organization loosely based on the ten-point program of the Black Panther Party. And he did eventually bring Stokely Carmichael to Nova Scotia to help organize the BUF. Rocky then went on to get a law degree and distinguish himself as an international human rights lawyer.

Rocky's more radical Black rights initiative remained a rarity in Canada in those days. And he quickly discovered that Canadians were firmly on his side when he was addressing the issue of the abuse of Black Americans; but when the focus was turned to Canada, most freedom-loving Canadians, particularly in the press, quickly lost interest or tried to hide the issue. This was most obvious in Rocky's part of the world, Halifax, where people began to fuss about Africville, the "American-style" Black ghetto on the edge of town. It is true that Africville, located on the south shore of the Bedford Basin, had virtually no services and an impoverished population, but it was a strong community. The solution to Africville's problems was for the larger society to provide it with the same services that were extended to all of the neighbouring white populations. But instead, against the fierce opposition of the people living there, the city expropriated all of the land and bulldozed the community to the ground. It was a startling example of Canada's traditional deaf ear and blind eye when dealing with Black Canadians.

Even though the number of Black Canadians was steadily increasing throughout the 1960s, with the largest influx coming from Jamaica and across the West Indies, it was clear that our place in Canada was not improving. In fact, we were losing ground. As our numbers increased, we became less of a novelty. We became visible, and very quickly we were seen first as threats and then as targets.

Around this time, local politics was also becoming fierce in a way it never had been in Toronto. The city was debating the proposed Spadina Expressway with Premier Bill Davis and the famous urbanist Jane Jacobs squaring off in the battle for the soul of the city. In the beginning, Jacobs and her Save Our City committee seemed to be a long shot. The expressway plans were already well developed and the city had purchased dozens of houses along the route for demolition. But there was a new wave of '60s-inspired defiance in Toronto and, finally, the Expressway proponents were forced to withdraw their plans. The city was left with those houses and no clue what to do with them. I stepped up and offered to rent a fifteen-room house for peanuts. The city accepted my offer. I furnished it with used furniture from the Sally Ann and quickly turned it into a second rooming house and filled it with students and young Americans escaping the draft. Eventually, the droves of Americans heading north were followed up by FBI agents, some of whom visited me to try and get information on my tenants or friends of my tenants. I had no reason to be impressed by these legal bounty hunters, and I recall using the F-word a few times in inviting them to get off of my property.

By this time, too, I had become a Canadian citizen. In fact, I had become a Canadian citizen the first chance I got after my minimum three years of permanent residency. The reason, I must admit, was not so much my blind love of country, but the knowledge that as a Black man swimming in these waters, I was vulnerable to all sorts of attacks that could easily end with deportation. This vulnerability is something that most white Canadians, I know, don't really understand. I reflected on this years later when I was having lunch with a bank manager and we were discussing Pierre Trudeau's political battles in getting acceptance for a Charter of Rights and Freedoms. The bank manager said he didn't care one way or another because he had always had his rights and he had no doubt that he always would. This was certainly not so for Black Canadians, women, political dissidents, Indigenous people, and the poor in Canada, but I had to agree with him that Canada did have a shining civil rights record when it came to protecting the rights of white bank managers.

By this time, I was increasingly struck by the entrepreneurial spirit — mainly from immediate need but also, I think, because I was now entering my thirties and I was looking ahead to a possible life after teaching. While I was still enjoying my rapport with students, my relations were not so sanguine with the management and more than once during this period I thought back to my father's admonition of never working for someone else. Even though I was on the run taking care of the rooming houses, I still found myself checking the newspapers every day for new business opportunities.

One finally caught my attention. A twenty-room private hospital at 682 Broadview was available to rent. I went to look it over. The property had been closed down and was in the hands of an accountant. But it was a sturdy building. Originally, it had been the family home of William Wesley Hiltz, who had been elected mayor of Toronto in 1924, although he served less than a year before getting turfed. Hiltz, I learned, was a militant Orangeman who had also started out as a teacher before going into the construction business. At one point during the transition, he would take his students out to the job site, give them shovels, and make them dig foundations. I resisted the urge to copy Hiltz by bringing my Forest Hill students down to do the renovations and instead brought in an accountant friend, Ron Hutchinson, and together we decided that a nursing home could be a much more profitable business than a rooming house because the province licensed the number of beds and subsidized some of the costs on a per-bed basis, with the client paying the balance.

The Donview Nursing Home opened in the spring of 1968. The business plan was solid, and I realized I had hit on a real need. The twenty beds were quickly filled. Six months later, when another small eighteen-bed nursing home went up for sale on Tyndall Avenue at Dufferin and King, I made an offer and opened the Tyndall Nursing Home. Suddenly I was operating thirty-eight nursing home beds. I would later learn that there was a flaw in the plan that made it necessary to rigorously manage costs, because under provincial rules it was impossible to evict clients who did not pay their fees. Certainly it was a compassionate law for those who found themselves unable to pay, and I never was concerned by carrying those who honestly couldn't afford the fees, but a number of well-off clients used their knowledge of the law to refuse to pay — knowing there was really nothing I could do about it. When I finally sold the two nursing homes, I was owed an uncollectible $100,000 by clients.

I was still teaching at Forest Hill all through this, but my teaching career was teetering on the edge. Even though I carried out my business ventures on my own time, as I began to have some success I could feel the attitude of my colleagues changing. At the time, it confused me. But I have since learned to identify a certain strain of Canadian racism by which more or less liberal whites will treat Black people well, as long as they perceive the Blacks to be beneath them on the social scale. But if a Black person is better off than they are, they can't handle it. These people will gladly give a you their old television, but if they see you have a better television than they do, they will resent the hell out of you. And this resentment was growing among my colleagues at Forest Hill.

I was not the only Black person at Forest Hill who experienced this. And the main problem was the school principal, who in reality was simply a teacher who got lucky in landing the job. A fellow teacher, Dr. George Bancroft, a Black from Guiana who had a Ph.D. in Education, was contacted by the landmark Hall-Dennis Committee on Education in Ontario and asked to do some research. He wanted to go to Winnipeg to take part in a study, which meant he would be temporarily absent from Forest Hill. For the collegiate, having such a respected international scholar on our staff was a great tribute to the school. But Bancroft was refused permission to take part in the study. It seemed to me that race was a major factor. From experience, I knew that white people did not like seeing Black people getting ahead.

About the same time, the school went through a change when Forest Hill village became part of Metropolitan Toronto. Previously, the Forest Hill School Board ran classes on a six-day cycle, which meant that on certain days I was finished school at 2:00 p.m. Then I could head off to my second workday, taking care of the rooming house and tackling the enormous amount of work it took to set up the nursing home. With the schedule change, the only day I could leave early was Friday, but my department head decided to block me from leaving by calling pointless Friday end-of-the-afternoon meetings that kept me at the school to the last bell, even though I had no classes to teach. He did this even before long weekends — anything to keep me from getting to my off-school work. Finally, I had enough. I went to the principal and told him I was not going to stay for any meetings called for the final hour before the long weekend. Or any Friday afternoon meetings. That put an end to the time-wasting meetings, but of course it did not end the resentment.

A teaching inspector was sent to review my class. At the outset, I explained to him where I was in the lesson plan. Because of lab and equipment use issues, the science teachers had staggered our lesson plans so I was one lesson ahead of one teacher and one behind the other. I explained this to the inspector, but when the review was made this was not mentioned and I was reprimanded for having fallen behind one lesson.

Frustrations were accumulating. I was called in to the principal's office for a chat. He asked me, point-blank, if I would rather be somewhere else. I asked him what he meant. He said he heard that I had refused to help a student. I knew who he was talking about and I gave him the name. It was one of my few goof-off students, the son of well-known surgeon, who I had arranged to help after class every afternoon for a week to bring him back up to speed. But the kid was so determined to waste his and his fellow students' time during the class, I told him: "That's it. You're wasting my time now, so I'm not going to waste my time helping you after class today." I was making a point. Now, the principal was using this to kick me in the shins.

I knew I was doing my job, and I still had a great rapport with my students — even with that goof-off surgeon's son — and teaching was still a pleasure for me. But the hostility from the principal and many of my fellow teachers was becoming increasingly unpleasant. I stood up and told the principal that maybe it was, after all, time that I moved on.

It was not easy, however. As I edged toward an exit,

I also felt the tug of the strong bond between me and my students and, by extension, their families. After gauging my support among students and parents and the local director of education, with whom I had become quite friendly, the principal quickly flipped around and tried to get me to stay. By this time my businesses were employing twenty-five people, and straddling the two careers had me running ragged. I wavered, but finally I screwed up my courage and left. Certainly with some sadness. But also with some pride in knowing that in the noble profession of teaching, I had made some positive difference in the lives of my students. I know they had a positive influence on mine.

In a sense, I was finally fulfilling my father's repeated admonition to work for yourself and not for other people. But unfortunately, he was not there to share this with. My mother was taking the recent deaths of her husband and her mother particularly hard. The same year they passed away, we lost my brother-in-law to a motorcycle accident; it was a devastating time for the family. I had scraped together all the money I had to visit my mother during Christmas break in 1963, but visits back were rare in those days.

My sister and brother were taking advantage of the recently relaxed immigration laws to move to Toronto for varying lengths of time, which was a real pleasure to me. But I also kept up my connection to Jamaica, where the political landscape was being shaken up by a new generation. Just as Canada in the late 1960s saw the rise of a new kind of politician in Pierre Elliott Trudeau, Jamaica saw the rise of Michael Manley, the flamboyant son of the more aloof Norman Manley. In fact, Michael Manley became a friend of Trudeau's, and like Trudeau he befriended Fidel Castro and the Cuban revolution. He also had an interesting tie to Canada: as soon as he turned eighteen in 1942, he headed north and joined the Royal Canadian Air Force to serve as an officer and pilot in Europe. After the war, he enrolled in the London School of Economics. Although he was there at the same time as Trudeau, they did not meet until much later, when they were prime ministers of their respective countries and worked together on a major reform of the Commonwealth.

We know that the U.S. authorities were worried about Trudeau during this period, fearing that his friendship with Castro and his opposition to the Vietnam war meant he was some kind of closet socialist. But Canada, as a NATO member and a charter member of the White People's Club, had certain built-in protections that Jamaica did not. When Manley allied himself with the Black Power movement in Jamaica and tried to address serious social problems with socialist measures, he was instantly set upon by the CIA. The interference increased dramatically when he tried to lead Jamaica into the Non-Aligned Movement. Jamaican elections became characterized by gunfire as the JLP took a hard right turn to oppose Manley's leftism, and seemed to have received a green light to shoot its way back into power if that's what it took to get rid of him.

Canada was not immune from political violence during this period. FLQ bombs and kidnappings transfixed and finally transformed the country as the separatist issue dwarfed all others. Indirectly, this would have a major impact on all minorities in Canada. The Royal Commission on Bilingualism and Biculturalism, set up in the 1960s to address the issue of Quebec nationalism, recommended adopting bilingualism at the federal level and establishing new supports for a bicultural Canada. But the immediate backlash against the francization of Canada, as it was seen in the west and in Southern Ontario, was linked to powerful constituencies: the old British Protestant Canada that had always mistrusted everything to do with the French and all "ethnics"; and the newcomers, the millions of Canadians who didn't trace their roots to the old British or French Canada. Trudeau still embarked on a bilingualism program in 1971, but to split the opposition he championed multiculturalism instead of biculturalism, using the catchphrase "The Just Society."

This new policy gave hope to Black Canadians, who had so long faced Canada's historically *unjust* society. But it would be a long time before that hope would be fulfilled.

Beginning in the 1960s, Toronto's influx of Black immigrants was housed in a new Jane-Finch high-rise ghetto created by the North York Planning Department. In less than a decade, the neighbourhood of 1,300 people exploded to a dense 33,000, mostly Black and other minority people. Today, this area is annually ranked the "least livable" in Toronto. Its high rate of police and lateral violence takes an enormous toll on Black youth. These issues were gradually rising to the fore in the mid-1960s, but Canadians were determined to look away. Our people today are still paying the price.

CHAPTER NINE

BUILDING A FAMILY,
BUILDING A BUSINESS

I was fortunate that, in the decade when the new wave of racism was beginning to break across Canada, I was not among the most vulnerable. By the late 1960s and early 1970s, I had business interests that allowed me some flexibility when I was dealing with banks, suppliers, clients, and competitors. Which isn't to say that I did not experience overt racism in the business world — I certainly did, and I will describe some of the incidents below — but I was less vulnerable than most, especially the new arrivals who were being kept poor and marginalized by employment discrimination.

Even from my somewhat protected position, I felt the stiffening of the winds of racism around 1968 when Carol and I were looking for a bigger apartment, and then a house to accommodate our growing family.

Our daughter, Nicole, was born in 1968 and, as it does for everyone, the arrival of our first child instantly transformed our lives. Like all new parents, we were suddenly working the twenty-four-hour baby shift and this was complicated for me when Carol went back to work evenings at the hospital a few nights a week while I looked after Nicole. Fortunately, Nicole was a delightful baby who turned into a delightful child and, finally, an adult who, after blazing her own trail, came back for a time to work with me in one of my most difficult projects, building a Black radio station. But all this was in the future, and during those early months our lives were broken into what seemed like very short units of feedings and diapers.

While Carol was pregnant, we had moved out of the one-bedroom apartment on Keele and into a nearby three-bedroom. Looking for that new place, I discovered that many of the available apartments I had called about on the phone were no longer available when I showed up in person. In a few instances, I had a white friend check later and the places were suddenly available again. This was not, of course, entirely new. I had run into this in Canada before, but what was new was the frequency. As the Black population of Toronto was steadily increasing, it seemed the racist population was increasing at a doubling rate.

By the end of 1970, when Carol was expecting again and we were looking for a house, the atmosphere was becoming openly hostile and there were sporadic news reports of violence against Blacks in Toronto and other large Canadian cities where our numbers were increasing. By this time, I knew well enough that the housing market in certain areas was closed to Blacks, so I asked my friend Jack Horsley, who had moved back from Sault Ste. Marie to Toronto to work as a city legal counsel, to buy the house in trust for me. He agreed. On the house search, he would identify himself as the purchaser, and I was introduced as the tradesman who would make renovations after it was purchased. It was something of a joke between the two of us — on the surface. But it was deeply frustrating to endure this level of racial discrimination.

The house that interested me was in a new development where you picked the lot you wanted, then chose from a number of house models to build on it. Jack went to the developer with our offer and the developer accepted it initially, until he understood that Jack was buying the house in trust. Jack didn't deny it, but he didn't say who he was purchasing the house for.

The developer looked him in the eye and said, "You have to tell me who the house is for. Otherwise I could end up selling to a Black family with twelve kids."

Nothing could have been clearer. Jack and I went to see Mortie Shulman, the flamboyant and crusading coroner turned NDP politician with a reputation for supporting civil and human rights causes. At the time, he was an MPP in the Ontario legislature and was in the news for defying Ontario's censorship of the book *The Happy Hooker* by selling it out of his office with a 10% MPP discount. So he did not sound like a guy who was going to accept blatant racial discrimination in the Toronto housing market.

Shulman was happy to support us and took our cause to the Ontario Human Rights Commission, which, unfortunately, at the time had a reputation as a lapdog rather than an attack dog. In the end, the commission bought the developer's rapidly backtracking contention that he was referring to the possible size of the family, not its race, and his later suggestion that he'd refused to sell to us because the house I'd chosen was too big for the lot. This was brought into question years later when a former commission employee told me that far the lot I had chosen, from being too small, now had a full-sized swimming pool in the back yard.

While the case was before the Human Rights Commission, I still had to find a place to live, and this became especially urgent after we discovered that we were expecting not one child but twins. We found a roomy house on Cassandra Boulevard, north of Lawrence Avenue, that had been put up for quick sale by an IBM employee who was being transferred to New York — and apparently he could care less who bought his house as long as he got the price he needed to get out of town. It turned out to be a good price, and I finally decided, against my lawyer's advice, not to take the original developer to court.

I had my hands full not only with work, which was entering a crucial phase, but with the arrival of the twins, Michael and Kevin. Sleep became a faint memory for me and Carol. We found that when we managed to get one of the boys to sleep, the other would wake up, and before he was asleep he would wake the other again. It was the same when one got sick. You would just about get him nursed back to health when the other would catch the same thing. It was an endless cycle of changing diapers, running the washing machine, and sterilizing bottles. And Nicole was then three years old with all the urgent demands three-year-olds can muster. It was a joyful but thoroughly exhausting period.

As the twins grew, a new concern arose: their development seemed to lag. After endless tests and speculation, they were diagnosed with fragile X syndrome, an abnormality in the X chromosome that leads to intellectual disability. In their case, it was a fairly mild form; they would both be what is called "high functioning." As adults, they can move around the city on their own. They are meaningfully employed in limited-ability occupations, one in maintenance, the other in a special needs program at George Brown College.

Despite their limitations in some areas, sports have played a big role in their lives and it has been a pleasure watching them develop. Their sport turned out to be hockey, and I hope you will excuse a short detour here to briefly outline the remarkable program of Special Hockey started by Pat Flick that has added so much to the lives of my sons and my family, and to thousands of others around the world. It is a story about fighting for fairness not in the area of race, but for those with disabilities, which is another cause I believe in deeply.

Pat Flick is the type of person that we all, at our best, aspire to be. His hockey initiative began in 1970, the year before my sons were born, when he was working at his job as a machinist during the week and coaching kids' hockey on the weekends at the Grandravine Arena on Keele Street. During the season, Pat noticed a young developmentally disabled boy who came to the rink every Saturday to watch his brother play. Pat finally went over and spoke to the boy, and it quickly became clear that he was not just there for his brother. He loved hockey, just like any other Canadian kid, but he was excluded because of his disability.

The idea of a Canadian kid deprived of hockey bothered Pat. He decided he had to do something about it. Speaking to the boy's parents, he learned of another boy in a similar position — outside the rink looking in — so Pat went to the Grandravine Athletic Association and asked them for free ice time. The association agreed and with those two kids he founded the Grandravine Tornadoes. And Special Hockey was born. Word spread and suddenly parents from across Toronto with special needs children were contacting him to ask if their kids could join. No one was refused.

The stories of Pat's successes are legendary. In one of the first seasons, he walked into the dressing room to find the father of one of his players in tears. Pat had done what the father had been trying to do for thirteen years: teach his special needs son to tie his own skates.

With his typical modesty, Pat explains: "We didn't treat them like the handicapped because I didn't know how to treat a handicap. So I figured I might as well treat them like hockey players."

My sons, with a lot stacked against them in other areas, took to Pat Flick's hockey program with great enthusiasm, and Special Hockey International has taken them to tournaments across North America and to Europe. The league is open to players from six to sixty, and my sons still play hockey today, in their forties. For me, the irony is that as a Jamaican-born cricketer, soccer player, and track and field guy who was never too impressed with hockey, Canada still managed to make the game an important part of my family's life. It really is a national religion, and Pat Flick was, for Special Hockey, the visionary and missionary who launched it and spread its influence around the world: it is now featured in the Special Olympics and is played by thousands of players internationally.

While our home life was busy with Nicole and the twins, things were also moving fast on the business front. With the additional time at my disposal after I left teaching, I was able to quickly expand the Tyndall Nursing Home from eighteen to thirty-six beds; with the twenty beds in the Donview home, I now had a total of fifty-six beds to operate, all while running the two rooming houses.

The big change for me came in 1972, when the provincial government brought in a whole slew of regulations for nursing homes that determined everything from the amount of floor space required for every bed to the number of wash basins, along with specific requirements for lighting, ventilation, and heating, as well as detailed new safety regulations. The measures were grandfathered in up to April 27, 1972, so I could have continued to operate my small, rudimentary homes, but the thinking behind the regulations — to improve the lives of nursing home patients — made sense, and I decided to try to consolidate and upgrade. I bought up three licences for a total of thirty-two beds from smaller operations and developed a plan for a new state-of-the-art facility.

This would require major capital — from a business point of view, a leap into the unknown, something I have been willing to do throughout my life. Since this was Canada in the 1970s, I would also have to do my business dealings through a white front man. With most delicate transactions, I generally worked with my friend and accountant and overall financial advisor, Irwin Siderson. Just as Jack Horsley had done in my house search, Irwin would make initial arrangements with white lenders and potential business partners.

For the new facility, I purchased an acre and a half of land in Mississauga at 1060 Eglinton Avenue, southwest of the airport. The lot had a tricky entrance because Little Etobicoke Creek ran through it. Another acre was for sale next door, and my plan was to buy this adjoining acre, give myself an easement to easily enter the original 1.5 acres, and then sell it at a profit. We successfully completed that deal and built our three-story facility as planned, with extra provisions such as additional kitchen and dining spaces as well as an additional elevator shaft roughed in to make it possible to add a fourth floor later. We then discovered that our finances were in order, and we did not have to sell the extra acre; we eventually built a fifty-seven-bed retirement home on the additional land. Gradually, we put together a continuum of care, a kind of seniors' village, and five years later we added the fourth floor to give us another forty-nine beds for a total of 151.

This was not, of course, a simple matter. From the beginning, the terrain was littered with financial and political land mines. Even the purchase of the additional licences was controversial because, at the time, licences were not supposed to be transferred between counties. One of my new licences came from Mississauga, but the other two came from Etobicoke and Bolton, and this flared onto the front pages of the newspapers when it was discovered that the Bolton transfer was from within Premier Davis's own riding. As soon as we weathered that storm, I submerged myself in the maze of new regulations that had to be met to construct the facility to the complex new code. This also meant cutting through the red tape to get approval for every element, and Irwin and I were often caught up in the sticky web of regulations. I can remember numerous times when we seemed to have been completely blocked from reaching the goal. But I couldn't afford to fail. I had sold off the rooming houses for investment capital; when we were stymied by the wall of bureaucracy, we had no choice but to back up and take another run at it — find a way through, or make one — and continue on.

One of the most unpalatable obstacles during this period was the kind of taunting racism I received from banks. It began with the $1.3-million mortgage I negotiated through my broker, Ernie Nock, to build the new facility. In the financial plan, I needed $300,000 in bridge financing to complete the package and it seemed like a done deal. I went to my bank, which I had been dealing with for twelve years, and I was stunned to find the door slammed in my face. I went to meet with Ernie, who had arranged the $1.3-million deal, to give him the bad news. Ernie said, flatly, that there was no business reason for the bank to turn down the bridge financing. We both knew what he meant. They were simply not going to lend money to a Black man. Ernie asked me for the name of the loans officer who had refused me, but he didn't go to see him. He went instead to the bank manager and told him that the decision of the loans officer made no business sense, and, if it wasn't reversed, his mortgage company would stop dealing with the bank in any future projects. In reviewing the financial application, the bank manager suddenly decided that it was a good business proposal and approved it over the head of his loans officer.

A few years later, when I discovered that it made sense to purchase a laboratory because we were spending so much on laboratory fees at the nursing home, I ran into more of the same from another bank. The laboratory deal was actually fairly complicated, involving the consolidation of two existing labs, Standard Medical Diagnostics and Ed Bec Paramedical, with my purchasing 51% of the new company. I was about to close the deal with the bank — which recognized that this was a smart move — when the bank manager said to me, "I don't mind dealing with you. I might not want you to marry my daughter, but I'll deal with you."

I had to stop for a moment to take in what he had just said.

"You won't have to worry about that," I said, "because it's obvious your daughter has a lousy pedigree."

Then I walked out and found another bank.

In some cases, banks reacted like the developer Jack Horsley and I had dealt with. When a later $3-million mortgage was coming due, and I was negotiating at a distance with a major international bank, all the details were worked out until I was ready to sign. I had a quick meeting with the head honcho to go over the final details. But when we met, I could tell he was surprised to find I was not white. And so I was not surprised the next day when he suddenly called to say the deal was off. With the mortgage due in three weeks another nursing home owner offered to help, but with an obviously predatory offer. "There's no fire sale here," I said, and I scrambled to find another lender.

My adventures with banks continued, but I had learned not to trust them or rely on them. I began to protect myself against their arbitrary power by spreading my business around. I began to do this especially after I took a call from the business loans officer at my primary bank on my car phone. This was during the 1970s when car phones were really mobile radio operations and quite rare, but I had purchased it because of the long commute in Toronto traffic. When I picked up the bank officer's call, he was surprised by the background noise.

"Where are you?" he asked.

"In my car," I said.

"You have a car phone!" It wasn't a question — it was a statement, and I knew as soon as I heard him that this would be trouble for me: here was another one of those whites who can be decent to you as long as they think you are worse off than they are. This was the note I caught in this banker's voice and I knew that he would not forgive me for having a car phone. I began to further diversify my banking interests after that.

Sure enough, a few months later, he tried to sabotage me. He said he was checking my account and saw that I was overdrawn and demanded that I make a payment on the account before 3:00 p.m. that day. This was it. He was going to show me who was boss. I let him know that I understood what he was up to by answering, "I'll show you that I am more of a man than you are. I'll bring you a bank cheque for the full amount this afternoon."

I went to the bank, deposited the cheque, and then went to the bank manager. I told him what had happened and said, "I don't want to deal with that guy ever again."

The bank manager hurriedly assured me that I wouldn't have to. He would administer my account himself if need be, and he would transfer my file away from the offending business loans officer immediately.

So I did get satisfaction, as I usually could in the business sphere — I had real assets, and in this system a certain power comes with capital. It doesn't make you at all immune from racism, but it does soften its effects in many ways. Still, I continued to do business understanding that, as a Black man, I was the hare surrounded by lions. I had to be eternally vigilant about where the lions were and the mood they seemed to be in.

Toronto, during the 1970s, was not at its best in race relations. As their population in the city increased to visible levels, Blacks found themselves confronted not only by blatant discrimination but by both random and organized violence.

The organized violence came first from the neo-Nazi white supremacist Western Guard Party. It had its origins in the Edmund Burke Society, a group made up of former

Nazis and extreme right wingers, many of Eastern European origin, who spent the 1960s battling the New Leftists, often by physically attacking them during demonstrations. In 1972, they merged with white supremacist groups like the Canadian wing of the Ku Klux Klan (which was burning crosses in Southern Ontario in the 1960s) to form the Western Guard. Its focus was on Blacks, Asians, and East Asians. As with the Nazis and Jews in the 1930s, Toronto's visible minorities were just numerous enough to be held up as a menace but few enough to be basically helpless against attacks. During the 1970s, it became clear that the hate groups were not growing in isolation. They were working to feed the growing wave of racism in Canada, but they were also feeding off it.

The Western Guard began with hate-filled propaganda: White Power graffiti on the walls of neighbourhoods with growing Black populations, and threats in pamphlets demanding an immediate end to "coloured" immigration, the "repatriation" of all non-whites in Canada, and the awarding of $1,000 to white parents at the birth of each white child. In the late 1970s, a Western Guard activist, James McQuirter, opened up a Canadian Ku Klux Klan office in the east end on Dundas Street, where there was a growing Black and East Asian community. His KKK branch came to national attention when it was found to be distributing "White Youth Corps" literature at Riverdale's Monarch Park Secondary School. Again, many Canadians would choose to see this as some kind of American import into Canada, particularly because the KKK is so profoundly associated with the American South. But it is interesting to read some of the KKK racial separatist literature of the period and to see what it was advocating. Far from being imports, the Western Guard, the KKKers, and the many who agreed with them were simply calling for the restoration of the long-standing Canadian policy of excluding all but a small token Black immigration.

The threats quickly escalated to real violence with random beatings of Blacks and other visible minorities on the streets, and disruptions of community meetings, at which crowds were attacked with mace. I was treasurer at the Jamaican Canadian Association at the time, and our headquarters on Dawes Road was burned to the ground. Because it wasn't insured, we were left for some time without a base and I had to lend the organization money and help arrange financing for a new building we purchased on Dupont Street near Bloor and Dundas.

One of the favourite Western Guard targets during this period was the Black newspaper *Contrast*, started in 1969 by Al Hamilton. It was one of the most important Black cultural institutions in Toronto from its founding at the end of the 1960s through to the late 1980s.

Al and I would become close friends and eventually collaborate on the paper when I became its owner and publisher. But Al would also shine as one of the city's most colourful characters. His ancestors were part of a very small group of free Blacks who managed to get into Canada in the 1850s to escape the federal Fugitive Slave Act, through which even freed Blacks could be put back into the bonds of slavery. Born in Edmonton, he grew up throughout the prairies, living in both Regina and Winnipeg, cities with very few Black families at the time. As a young man, he moved to Toronto with his wife and son and made a living first as a performer in his own theatrical company and then as publisher of *Contrast*.

The first issue of the paper came out on February 15, 1969, and focused on the battle at Sir George Williams University in Montreal, where Black students and their supporters, after more than a year of fighting overt racism at the university, held a sit-in at the computer building. The room was set on fire when the police attacked. Black students were expelled, jailed, and deported as a consequence of these events, and *Contrast* was there to give the students and all Canadian Blacks a voice. What is called the Sir George Williams riot was recently covered in Mina Shum's documentary *Ninth Floor*, but in the 1970s it was *Contrast* that informed the world about what exactly happened, and why, from the inside. From that point on, *Contrast* became known as the "eyes, ears, and voice" of the Black community across Canada.

This visibility put the newspaper under constant threat from the Western Guard thugs, and clearing the building for bomb threats became part of the weekly routine. But Al was unflinching, and he never backed down from defending Blacks and attacking racism in Toronto, Canada, and internationally.

The rising tide of racism and the violent activities of the white supremacist and anti-Semitic organizations was sparking concern throughout minority communities. In

May 1975, a group of Torontonians met at a downtown restaurant to discuss "the increasing frequency of hate-motivated violence against African and South Asian Canadians in Toronto's streets, subways, and shopping plazas." The group, led by local trade union leaders, included Sam Fox of the Metro Labour Council, Terry Meagher of the Ontario Federation of Labour, two members of the Social Planning Council of Metro Toronto, Ben Kayfetz of the Canadian Jewish Congress, and Wilson Head, the Black representative. He had moved from the U.S. to Canada in 1959, bringing a lifetime of experience in civil rights activism with him, and had served as director of Toronto's Social Planning Council before moving on to pursue his academic interests at York University.

At this meeting, the Urban Alliance on Race Relations was founded, and Head was made executive director. The UARR set as its goal partnerships with law enforcement and government to try to turn back the tide of racism in Toronto. It would also work to maintain stable, peaceful, and harmonious relationships among the various racial and ethnic groups within the Greater Toronto community. Its board of directors was to be an alliance of ordinary citizens who would reflect the diversity of modern society in Toronto and Canada at large. This was an undeniably well-meant and perhaps important first step, but the UARR was not able to respond to what was coming. Toronto was turning into a petri dish of toxic relations, and relations between minority communities and the police were about to be seriously infected.

The first flashpoint came during one of those hot, humid Toronto nights in August when you could almost feel you were in the West Indies. The streets were full of people, and music pounded out of the open windows of the clubs. The police, increasingly accused of their own abuse of Black citizens, were called to the Flying Disco, a club at King and Bathurst, for what sounded like a typical dispute between the bouncer and a couple of bar patrons. The patrons, it turned out, were twenty-four-year-old Nova Scotia Black Andrew "Buddy" Evans and his brother. Their dispute with the club bouncer had begun the previous night when the bouncer, according to Buddy's brother, had threatened them with a knife. So, on this night Buddy had brought a knife wrapped in a garbage bag, in case the bouncer pulled a knife on them again.

The bouncer saw them coming. He called the police. Within minutes, Evans was confronted by two young officers. Constable John Clark stated that Evans (who at no time had even removed the knife from the bag) had grabbed the nightstick out of his hand and threatened him with it at close range. When Evans failed to respond to a warning, Clark fired the fatal shot. But as an article about the case in the *Osgoode Law Journal* pointed out, "this story was contradicted by numerous witnesses who swore that Evans had clearly surrendered before Clark fired, that he had dropped the nightstick, and he was standing with his arms raised." What happened next only added fuel to the fire. A swarm of other police came onto the scene and hustled the shooter, Constable Clark, to the hospital because he seemed faint, leaving Buddy Evans bleeding to death unattended.

Those who had witnessed the killing immediately shouted abuse at the police for the cold-blooded killing of an unarmed man. To try and quell the increasingly restive crowd, the local precinct officer sent two Black officers onto the scene. Recognizing that the Black officers were being used as tokens to buy them off, people became angrier at them than they were at the white policemen. One officer began fighting with a bystander who he said was threatening a fellow officer. Fights broke out between Blacks when one would lunge in fury toward an officer and another, to prevent further violence, would grab him and try to pull him back.

A riot warning was hastily given, and police from across downtown flooded into the area to drive the bystanders away. But by then, nothing could stop the outrage over the killing, which quickly came to symbolize all of the abuse and brutality that Canadian Blacks had suffered at the hands of police and racist groups over the previous decades.

A protest rally the next day attracted more than 1,200 demonstrators, mainly Toronto Blacks who had simply had enough and were demanding that the police officer who shot Buddy Evans be charged with murder, or at the very least that an inquest into the killing be held.

I shared the outrage of the crowd, and I was glad to see that at last people were not taking it lying down. In the days after the Buddy Evans shooting, I called my friend Bromley Armstrong and *Contrast* editor Al Hamilton, and then I called Jean Augustine and Charlie Roach and I said, "Let's meet — we have to do something."

They all agreed. I was especially glad to have Jean Augustine with us. Jean had arrived in Canada from

Me and the Honourable Jean Augustine.

Grenada in the late 1950s as a domestic and had worked to put herself through the University of Toronto for an education degree. When I met her, she was a school principal and active in promoting Black rights in a number of organizations. In the 1990s, she would run for the Liberals and become the first Black woman elected to the House of Commons, and later the first appointed to a federal Cabinet position as the Minister of State for multiculturalism and the status of women, and — at the end of her career — the first Black woman to serve as deputy speaker in the House of Commons.

In his own way, Charlie Roach would make an equally important contribution. He was the son of a Trinidadian trade union organizer who arrived in Canada the same year as me, in 1955, as an aspiring priest studying theology at the University of Saskatchewan. But he says he was politicized by the times, and, in the late 1950s, he came to Toronto to study law. In the 1960s, he worked as a lawyer for the city while he organized and participated in civil rights marches.

Accepting an award at the University of Toronto with my daughter,
Nicole, and human rights lawyer, Charlie Roach.

He opened a law firm in 1968; among his clients were asylum seekers from the U.S., including Black Panthers seeking refuge from prosecution. He also represented domestic workers facing deportation.

The result of the meeting was the creation of the Committee for Due Process, with all of us kicking in money to hire a lawyer to ensure that the killing of Buddy Evans wasn't simply swept under the rug, as seemed to be the goal of the police and press in the initial handling of the case. We got Jack Pinkofsky, a criminal lawyer with a street fighter reputation.

Due Process Committee members also began to meet with members of our own community to raise additional funds and to build support for our demand for charges against police, or at least an inquest over Buddy's killing. I was surprised that some in the Jamaican Canadian community were prepared to shrug off the killing because Buddy wasn't a Jamaican or even a West Indian. I reacted to this with some impatience. The police, I pointed out, did not ask Buddy where he was from before they shot him. He was a Black man — that was enough for them, and it had to be enough for us when we defended him.

This issue, the existence of a kind of sectarianism in the Black community, was one that would come up again and again in our attempts to build unity among our communities, with Trinidadians not wanting to cooperate with Jamaicans or Jamaicans with Grenadians. And it was especially strong when it came to West Indians and what we referred to as native Blacks. Perhaps because I had firsthand experience of how beaten down the Nova Scotia Blacks were, I had instant sympathy for Buddy Evans, who would have come to Toronto to escape the segregationist abuse in his home province, and I tried to explain this to my Jamaican friends and colleagues.

Largely because of our lobbying, individually and through the Due Process Committee, and with *Contrast* keeping the issue in front of the people every week, the government was forced into holding an inquest into Buddy Evans' killing. It turned into the longest inquest in Ontario's history, lasting eleven weeks and costing $200,000. In the end, the all-white jury decided that racism was not the motivating issue because, typically, they believed the police version of what had happened rather than the numerous eye witnesses who clearly stated that Buddy Evans was defenceless when he was shot. In this way, the inquest served not as an instrument of justice but as another important indicator of how things were stacked against us. In a just world, the killing should have resulted in a second degree murder charge against the police shooter; instead, the system completely absolved the police.

The next day, the press quoted me as calling the inquest report "a judicial abortion" because it extinguished any hope of justice for Buddy Evans. I was immediately criticized for this by members of the business community, including my bank manager, but I didn't care. As someone with his own business, I could speak out when others had to be silent. And I was determined to speak out. I always felt that to acquiesce to injustice is to share in it, and I was not going to hold my tongue.

Sadly, the issue of police violence against Blacks and other minorities was not going to go away. The killings kept happening. Within a year, thirty-five-year-old Albert Johnson, a father of four, was gunned down in his rooming house in the Vaughan/Oakwood area. This time, the two police were charged with manslaughter.

Again, the Black community was outraged. Two thousand people marched from Johnson's rooming house to the thirteenth division police headquarters to protest his killing. In the aftermath, another Black activist, Dudley

Laws, formed the Albert Johnson Defence Committee Against Police Brutality. The committee made three demands in its struggle for justice. First, that the killers, constables Inglis and Cargnelli, be charged with murder instead of manslaughter. Second, that Toronto police provide full compensation to Johnson's wife and four children — to help support them, the committee also set up the Albert Johnson Family Fund. Third, that the province and Ontario Attorney General Roy McMurtry establish an independent civilian review board for complaints against the police.

At the constables' trial, a pathologist testified that Johnson was likely kneeling or crouching at the foot of the staircase when he was shot. Because of the angle at which the bullet entered his stomach, and the fact that it then travelled downward, it was asserted that he was shot from above and was unlikely to have been posing an immediate threat to police. One of Johnson's children testified that her father was kneeling and shot execution-style. Despite the testimony of both Johnson's daughter and the pathologist, constables Cargnelli and Inglis were both acquitted of the crime.

But these police killings were the tip of an iceberg of harassment, abuse, and rampant discrimination plaguing the lives of Blacks in Toronto and throughout Canada in the 1970s — with the great majority of Blacks facing an increasingly hostile climate that was denying them jobs, business opportunities, and the full range of services provided to white Canadians. The centuries-old white Canada was fighting back at every opportunity against the arrival of Blacks and other races in their midst. This fight is still going on today. Although finally we have had some success in confronting it, we must continue to denounce the injurious stereotypes that were used, and still are, to try to keep Blacks at the bottom of the heap in Canada.

CHAPTER TEN

STEPPING UP: BLACK BUSINESS AND PROFESSIONAL ASSOCIATION

During the 1970s, Black Canadians were struggling to be heard, to take our place in Toronto as full citizens with an equal right to be in this country. One limited but still very real way we were able to assert ourselves was through Toronto's annual Caribana Festival. The festival began in 1966 with a group of friends — George Lowe, a land surveyor for the city; town planner Peter Marcelline; Dr. Alban Liverpool; dentist Maurice Bygrave; and Charles Roach — getting together to form the Caribbean Cultural Committee, which was later joined by Romain Pitt and several others. What they proposed was a 1967 centennial project that would celebrate Canada through West Indian culture, to be held on the Toronto islands. Their goal was modest, to attract "a larger crowd than usual" to the islands for the weekend celebration.

The event, held in early August 1967, was a smashing success, attracting a record crowd of 32,000 ferry users to the islands on Saturday, August 6 — which was also the sixth anniversary of Jamaica's independence — to the point where the festival was extended one day and attracted a new record of 35,000 the next day. This first Caribana was the largest-drawing centennial event held in Toronto that year, and its success persuaded the Governor General of Jamaica, Sir Clifford Campbell, to cancel his trip home from Montreal's Expo 67 so he could swing by Toronto to attend the Sunday event.

Caribana has gone on to become North America's biggest street festival and biggest Caribbean festival. Its final parade attracts a million attendees, and the overall festival attendance is typically around two million. I attended most of the early festivals and for many years I hosted an after-party at my house. Unfortunately, the party became too successful with friends of friends showing up to the point where the house and yard were packed and I knew less than half of the people there. When people I had never met began complaining that I was late serving the food, I realized it was time to give the after-party a rest.

Even today, with its tremendous success, Caribana remains dramatically underfunded by governments and is perennially teetering on financial collapse, despite the fact that it is almost completely reliant on volunteer labour. A few years ago, the festival won the sponsorship support of the Bank of Nova Scotia, but for our community Caribana's success has been bittersweet. The festival's more than $400 million impact on the city shows how important our community is to Toronto, but it also shows how little the municipal, provincial, and federal authorities care.

The lesson Torontonians seemed to take from Caribana in the 1970s was that we might be able to put on a party, but we were still basically "foreigners" in their overwhelmingly white city and country. One of the tools we tried to provide them with was knowledge through our promotion of Black History Month, inspired by the movement that had spread across the U.S. in the 1960s. In Toronto it was first proposed in 1978 by a group of Black educators in the Black History Society of Ontario. They pressed the city council to declare Toronto's first Black History Month, and they succeeded in February 1979. It would be sixteen years before Black History Month expanded across the country, thanks to a bill presented by Jean Augustine in the House of Commons.

The purpose of the month was straightforward. As the event organizers pointed out, "[W]ith roots dating back to 1603, African Canadians have defended, cleared, built and farmed this country; our presence is well established, but not well-known." The celebration of Black History Month was intended "to have the achievements of Black people recognized and told. As a nation with such diversity, all histories need to be known, all voices need to be expressed. One needs traditional history to engender a common culture; one needs Black history to engender a clearer and more complete culture." From the beginning, the organizers looked forward to the day when Black History Month would be unnecessary: "When the contributions of people of

African descent are acknowledged, when the achievements of Black people are known, when Black people are routinely included or affirmed through our curriculum, our books and the media, and treated with equality, then there will no longer be a need for Black History Month."

Toronto can take a certain pride in recognizing Black History Month so many years before the rest of the country did. But its embrace was not exceedingly warm. I experienced this when I was invited by a bank to speak to its employees during one of the early Black History Months. I was happy to do it. I spent some time preparing for the event, and, having faced outright racism from Toronto banks, I congratulated the manager on his foresightedness in encouraging greater cultural understanding of Blacks among its employees. That is until I arrived at the bank and I discovered that the talk I was to give was not in the boardroom but in the lunch room, while employees were moving in and out, opening and closing the fridge and eating their sandwiches. I was not there to bring serious issues to them, but instead to serve as a kind of background noise during lunch break while the bank recorded the event in their newsletter to give themselves an appearance of addressing the issue. I told the manager no thanks, and left.

One challenge we faced during this period was engaging our young people, especially those who found themselves exiled into what was rapidly becoming a high-rise ghetto in the Jane-Finch area. Then, as now, it was one of the most poorly serviced neighbourhoods in Toronto, with lack of green space and recreational facilities, and an astoundingly high unemployment rate that made escape almost impossible for most. In the hope of getting something going for the kids in the summer, I went to see some of the organizers of the then-abandoned Black Games, a local track and field meet. Working with them, and with another group that had tried a similar activity, and with Jean Augustine, we launched the Harriet Tubman Games, a two-day summer track meet for Toronto kids who didn't have the luxury of spending the summer in cottage country.

We chose Harriet Tubman as our namesake because she represented true heroism. Born into slavery in the early nineteenth century in the American South, she had freed herself then had gone on to lead more than a dozen groups into Canada in the Underground Railroad. She was renowned for packing a pistol that she said she was prepared to use on anyone who tried to recapture her people. She later helped John Brown recruit men for his raid on Harpers Ferry, and struggled for women's suffrage in the post-war era. A selfless fighter, Harriet Tubman was the type of symbol our kids needed in their own battles with a society that was too often hostile to them.

We planned to hold the first games at Birchmount Stadium, but we were met with stiff opposition rather than assistance from the city. When we told the Stadium overseers that we were going to go ahead and hold the games anyway, they continued to fight us — even after the games began, they threatened to padlock the park on the second day. On my way to the park that morning, I stopped off at a tool rental store to rent the largest bolt cutter I could find in case the park officials carried through with their threat. Fortunately, I didn't need it. The park was open and we were inundated with kids from all over the city, delighted to have the excitement of two days of track and field events in the beautiful July sunshine with picnic lunches in the shade. We had boys and girls of all ages, and no one was refused participation. It was two days of great amateur sport, in the real sense of amateur — for the sheer joy of it. Over the years, the games took on a higher profile when great Canadian stars like Donovan Bailey helped with the organizing, and eventually they attracted athletes from as far away as Trinidad.

Without really noticing it, as the 1980s began, social activism was taking up more and more of my time. But during this period I was still trying to move things forward in my business.

With the growing number of residents at Tyndall, I found there was a shortage of motels and hotels nearby for visiting out-of-town family members. I had continued to buy real estate in Mississauga, and I had an acre of land at Tomken and Eglinton. I purchased an easement from Gulf Oil to get direct access from Eglinton, and in 1990 I built a sixty-five-room hotel that I called Jolly Inn. A year later, I acquired the Days Inn registration, name, and reservation system. I ran the hotel into the late 1990s, and sold when I was raising cash for the radio station.

When the province froze up new nursing home beds, I explored the American market with the purchase of Woodhaven Manor, a 120-bed facility in Dallas. I kept it for

Sailing my yacht, the Jolly Dolphin, *in Montego Bay, Jamaica.*

two years, but it turned out to be more trouble than it was worth. One thing was the fires. We started having room fires during the daytime and in one of them a gentleman died, although the coroner ruled it wasn't the fire that killed him, but a heart attack. The mysterious and very worrisome fires continued, and this, along with the fact that I was getting worn down from the travel, led to me selling the place. It was a couple of years later that I received a courtesy call from the FBI in Dallas letting me know that they had caught the employee who was lighting the fires. She had left her job at Woodhaven for a local hospital, and when the same kind of mattress fires began to occur there the police put two and two together. Another one for the list of strange and inexplicable human obsessions.

My other offshore adventure was more whimsical, but no more successful. It was a day sailer tourist boat I bought in the mid-1970s. I had the idea for this when I went to Barbados on a family vacation and took a day cruise in a boat called the *Jolly Roger*. The name caught my attention for obvious reasons, and the fun of being on those topaz Caribbean seas with rum and great food and music made me think, Why don't I introduce this sort of sailing attraction to Jamaica? After a long search, I found a boat in Stuart, Florida, and set up a business out of Montego Bay. But the venture didn't last, mainly because of poor management on site and the impossibility of my doing proper oversight from Toronto. But I soon discovered that the business was harder, and costlier, to get out of than it was to get into. It was also attracting the type of people I wanted to stay away from, namely U.S. Drug Enforcement Administration people.

After the boat charter business was wound down, I had the boat at the West Indies Sugar Company's docks in Savanna-la-Mar where my brother-in-law, Levi McGregor, was the company general manager. I was anxious to sell it and didn't much care who bought it. I placed an ad in numerous Caribbean newspapers, including one in Colombia, and I think maybe this is what the American undercover narcotics agent saw, because he started calling me on a regular basis claiming to be interested in the boat. Finally, he decided to fly all the way up to Toronto to meet me at the Library Bar at the Royal York Hotel. I assumed it was because he wanted to close the deal on purchasing the boat — as was discussed on the phone.

But when we met at a quiet table near the back of the bar, he offered what sounded like a partnership where he said he could "make me rich" by using the boat to run drugs in the West Indies. He outlined in detail how payments would work from the first trip to the second trip, etc., but always adding, "I will make you rich!"

It occurred to me right away that a drug smuggler would not suddenly start chatting about his business to a stranger in a bar in a foreign country, and I had no question then and certainly no question now that this was an attempt at entrapment by a law enforcement agent. So I was careful to respond each time by saying, "I don't want to get rich."

But he persisted until I finally said, "If you are going to pay me so much money why don't you just buy the boat? It would be far cheaper for you."

He would then return to the same theme. "I'm going to make you rich."

And I would respond again: "I don't want to get rich."

He persisted, even drawing a silly scheme, saying that it was a big, roomy boat and it was also a pleasure craft so I could pull into a port and pretend to be partying. They would load it up with the drugs on the quiet and I would continue the fake partying into the dead of night and then, at some point, take off for a chosen destination. I said to him, "But the boat would still be registered in my name."

He finally realized I was not falling for this, and we parted company. I never heard from him again, but this encounter made me even more eager to sell.

I decided to sail it back to Florida myself to sell it there. But again, it would not be so easy to get rid of.

During the voyage, I encountered a storm off the Grand Cayman with forty-foot waves that caused serious damage and very nearly sank us. I put into George Town for repairs.

After the boat was docked in the Cayman for a year, I decided to get a Caymanian crew to make the final move back to Miami. But we had more bad luck with heavy seas, high winds, and more damage. The crew had to put into Cuba, of all places, with an American registered vessel. The good news was that because the crew were all Caymanians, I was able to get the British consulate to represent me, and Fidel gave them food and material for repairs — although I did have to pay for the soldiers who guarded them, or held them in custody, depending on how you looked at it. Then they finally sailed to Miami where the boat was sold at a discount. Even with a loss, I was happy to get out of the day cruise business.

In Toronto, our community was being buffeted by other kinds of storms, and the message that Blacks were not welcome in Canada even bubbled through the mainstream media. In one of the most blatant examples, a radio host of a jazz program on one of Toronto's most popular private radio stations casually remarked on air during Caribana that he would stay away from downtown Toronto that week because there were 400,000 Blacks on the streets. Except he didn't use the word Blacks, he used the N-word. When people in the Black community expressed their disgust at the man and the station, the announcer was merely reassigned, not even fired. That is what we were dealing with in Toronto in those days: eruptions of both organized and disorganized racism.

It was in this atmosphere that I was watching the late-night news on television at the end of September 1982, and I saw the opening ceremonies of the Commonwealth Games in Brisbane, Australia. I noticed as Team Canada entered the stadium that a large number of the athletes were Black. As I watched the games over the next few evenings, I saw that Mark McKoy, Milton Ottey, and Angella Taylor, to name just a few, were bringing gold to Canada while Blacks in Toronto were dodging racial attacks.

At the same time, I was hearing from younger and newly arrived Black business and professional men and women that they were being stymied at every turn. They were faced with all sorts of ugly stereotypes about Blacks and finding all sorts of roadblocks put in their way from potential sources of capital, service providers, and even clients.

With this thought, and the thought of the excellent athletes representing Canada on the field that I had been watching in the Commonwealth games, I called Bromley Armstrong and Al Hamilton to sound them out on the idea of forming some kind of association of Black business and professional people and, at the same time, honouring male and female Black athletes who were making Canada, for the first time since Harry Jerome's retirement, a force to be reckoned with in international track and field. Bromley and Al were encouraging, so I wrote a letter outlining the plan and sent it to a wide range of established figures in the Black community, inviting them to a founding meeting at the Underground Railroad restaurant on October 21. After the divisions I had seen in the Black community when we were organizing the Committee for Due Process for Buddy Evans, I made sure that there were Blacks from a range of countries, as well as native Blacks. The response was almost

Me at the Black Business and Professional Association in 1982.

universally positive with only a few exceptions, like the University of Toronto professor who objected to using the term "Black." To these few I was respectful, but I knew that getting tied up in semantics right off the bat was a way to ensure that nothing at all would come of the venture. I let the quibblers know that they were welcome to join with us — or not.

That initial letter was straightforward:

Dear Friend,

Re: Toronto's Black Business and Professional Persons

The time has come for us to assert ourselves in this society. We have among us "blushing unseen" some of the greatest minds in the world. These abilities and potentials must now be realized in the fullest, for our sake, and for our children's sake. This then is an inaugural meeting to discuss, organize, plan, and concentrate our efforts as a group of business and professional people . . .

One love,
Den Jolly

The choice of the Underground Railroad for our meeting was an obvious one. The restaurant was Toronto's first to specialize in American soul food and one of the few symbols of Black business success in the city. It had been founded in 1969 by two former Argonauts football stars, quarterback John Henry Jackson and kicker Dave Mann, and by Howard Matthews, the husband and manager of the great actress and blues singer Salome Bey.

A sense that the timing was right for the Business and

Professional Association was confirmed at that first meeting when about twenty-five people showed up, virtually everyone who I had invited. They included, to my great satisfaction, Harry Gairey, the father of Black resistance in Toronto; as well as Charlie Roach; Dr. George Bancroft; Al Mercury; Alvin Curling; and my friend Romain Pitt, then a lawyer but later an Ontario Superior Court judge, who chaired the meeting. When he gave me the floor, I spoke about the negative stereotypes plaguing Toronto Blacks, which were unpalatable enough for us to deal with, but even more injurious toward our young people. A Black business and professional association could put our collective weight behind defending and supporting our besieged community, as well as supporting scholarships and merit awards for the young.

I remember a buzz of excitement in the room: this was an idea whose time had come. In *Contrast* the next week, the event was heralded as a major step forward for the community under the headline: "Underground Luncheon Signals a New Era."

The initial plan was to organize a gala in March 1983 that would also serve as both a fundraising and friend raising event for the powerful political people we needed to help our community. At the same time, the evening's focus would be on honouring the Black athletes who had excelled at the Commonwealth Games: Angella Taylor, Ben Johnson, Mark McKoy, Milt Ottey, Tony Sharpe, and Desai Williams. We would then invite Harry Jerome to be the keynote speaker and to present the awards.

Harry had already become an important symbol for Canadian Blacks. As my good friend Fil Fraser wrote in his

Jerome biography *Running Uphill*, "Harry had matured into a respected teacher and an advocate for athletic youth development. After a challenging life in athletics, he was now beginning to take firm stands in the promotion of racial equality."

Fil went on to describe "the unique and powerful mental and emotional tool kit" that Harry Jerome had to develop to overcome adversity, his "extraordinarily powerful sense of discipline, a spartan practice of keeping his troubles to himself, and a near-superhuman work ethic."

One of Harry's greatest challenges, Fil pointed out, was a particularly Canadian brand of racism.

> Our Canadian barriers were more subtle than those
> south of the border, but the result was just as harsh;
> in some ways more so, because the image our country
> projected, an image in which so many of us tried so
> hard to believe, was of an open, egalitarian, non-
> racist society. In the United States, discrimination was
> usually open and often legally sanctioned; you knew
> exactly where you stood. In Canada . . . people rarely
> told you outright that you were not wanted. Your
> job application would be graciously accepted, but
> you would never get a call back; apartment buildings
> advertising vacancies were suddenly fully rented
> when you showed your face or revealed your name.
> In one study, researchers wrote seeking reservations
> from exclusive resorts. When they used Anglo-Saxon
> names, acceptance was almost automatic. But when
> the requests came from individuals with "foreign-

sounding" names, "No Vacancy" signs popped up almost everywhere . . .

All minorities still need a Swiss-army-knife, ready-for-anything, intellectual, and particularly emotional, survival kit: a thick skin to walk away from barriers you know are, at least in the short term, insurmountable; a quick wit to talk your way out of situations when you are cornered; fast feet to run when you have to; fast fists for when you cannot, or will not run; the fortitude to challenge discrimination when you can; and above all, *above all,* to counter the self-sabotaging sense of inferiority that too often lurks hidden in the deepest corners of your being, an unshakable belief in your own value as a human being.

White Canadians, Fil noted, tended to downplay, question, or marginalize Harry Jerome and his world-shattering achievements. But not Canada's Black community. "To members of Canada's Black community, Harry Jerome was an unblemished hero — one of its greatest role models." This was not only because of his achievements on the track, but because we knew that when Harry finished setting records in world capitals, back in Canada he was one of us, fighting our fight.

The invitation went out and Harry, to our delight, accepted. We went full speed ahead and booked the Harbour Castle Hotel ballroom.

Our delight quickly turned into shock and sadness when Harry Jerome died suddenly of a brain seizure on

December 7, 1982, at the age of only forty-two. It was a devastating loss.

With his tragic death, we knew that our first evening to celebrate Black achievement in Canada had to be in Harry Jerome's honour. I think it was Hamlin Grange who suggested we name the awards after him. This was immediately accepted. By then we had a founding board that included me, serving as president, and Grange, Al Mercury, Cindy Reeves, Jean Augustine, Bromley Armstrong, and Al Hamilton as board members. Once again, the board had been put together with an eye to promoting greater unity among the Black diaspora. All of our people. I was and still am convinced that nothing to which we aspire individually will allow us to move forward as a people. We have to work together.

We had a measure of how respected Harry Jerome was in the Black community and how badly our people wanted something, anything, to celebrate, when 1,200 people showed up at the Harbour Castle Hotel for our first function on March 5, 1983. We had worked to make the dinner as inclusive as possible of our community members — and the high attendance rate showed we had had considerable success — but we also found that this event became a major draw for politicians at all levels of government, from city councillors right up to the prime minister, fishing for support among Black community leaders that they could later turn into votes. In the longer term, this also helped our people gain access to the country's leadership in that Canadian power-brokering way.

The keynote speech was given by Howard McCurdy in his pull-no-punches stand-up style. Harry Jerome's daughter,

Harry Jerome's daughter, Debbie; me; and his wife, Wendy Jerome.

Debbie Jerome-Smith, spoke movingly. Looking back at the newspaper coverage, I see I was quoted as describing the evening as "glamorous, euphoric, and uplifting."

I gave the closing remarks, thanking the committee members; the emcee Bob Payne; and the designer of the award hardware, Herman Bristol. The evening ended with the great jazz singer Amanda Ambrose singing the unofficial Black anthem, "Lift Every Voice and Sing."

As mentioned, the honourees at the first Harry Jerome Awards dinner were the six Black Canadian athletes who excelled at that year's Commonwealth Games. In subsequent galas, the Black Business and Professional Association (BBPA) began recognizing outstanding Black Canadians in four main categories: Academic, Arts, Athletic, and Community Service; by 2011, there were

Me and award recipient P.K. Subban of the Montreal Canadiens at the Harry Jerome Awards.

sixteen awards in total.

In addition to the Harry Jerome Awards, the BBPA would go on to sponsor a national scholarship fund, first called the Harry Jerome Scholarship Fund, providing financial support to Black Canadian youth pursuing higher education. By 2010, the fund awarded close to fifty scholarships each year and built an endowment fund of close to $600,000. In the last twenty-four years, the fund has granted over 650 scholarships totalling close to $2.5 million.

I must admit it is with satisfaction that I have watched this organization grow from the meeting at the Underground Railroad to an organization that can offer so many Black people in all walks of life a sense of pride in their community in a system that sometimes seems designed to ensure they have zero self-esteem. We had to make sure that young Black people in Toronto knew that even though the system was erecting barriers in their paths, their community was behind them and, when necessary, shoulder to shoulder with them. It was painful to watch young people who did not recognize that they were being discriminated against and instead blamed themselves and attacked themselves. Discrimination and racism can truly make you sick, as the anger against the injustice is turned inward.

At the same time, while the BBPA awards remain the most prestigious Black awards in Canada, and they are still popular community events, I believe they have lost their way somewhat in a political sense, as they are often used for the self-promotion of the leadership rather than as a service to the community. One symptom of their decline is that Debbie Jerome-Smith, who made the trip from Edmonton every year to attend, recently stopped going because she felt the leadership had forgotten who she was. Then, when Fil Fraser published his remarkable book on Jerome, the organizers refused to even mention it at the gala. Today, the leadership's push to put themselves in the limelight too often involves elbowing others out of the way. I experienced this myself during the thirtieth anniversary of the organization in 2012 when not only was I not invited to play a role in the celebration, I was shuffled off to the far reaches of the room with a table near the back wall. The organization had forgotten its founders, and I left the hall.

In the early 1980s, Canada's Black communities were still struggling to build their own institutions and to ensure themselves a voice in the larger one. Most were fighting at the community level, but an increasing number went into mainstream politics, albeit with mixed results.

The first Black man to run in a federal election in Canada was William White, a musician and composer living in Toronto. He came from my old university town of Truro, where he grew up with his famous sister, the concert singer Portia White. In 1949, William ran for the Co-operative Commonwealth Federation in the Spadina riding and came a respectable third with just under 6,000 votes.

Nineteen years later, Lincoln Alexander was elected as a Progressive Conservative MP of a Hamilton riding, becoming the first Black man to win a seat in Parliament. Lincoln was born in Toronto, but his family had West Indian roots, with his mother from Jamaica and his father, a CPR porter, from St. Vincent and the Grenadines. After spending some time in Harlem as a child, he enlisted in the RCAF during the war and afterward attended Osgoode Hall Law School. After his success in the 1968 election, Lincoln went on to trailblaze as the first Black cabinet minister and, finally, in 1985, as the first Black Lieutenant Governor of Ontario or any province.

While Lincoln's career path to power often seemed designed to make as few waves as possible, the same cannot be said of Canada's second Black MP, Howard McCurdy. Howard was born in London, Ontario, and attended Western University on the road to what was a groundbreaking academic career. He was awarded his master of science and a Ph.D. in microbiology and chemistry from Michigan State University, and in 1959 he joined the biology department at Assumption University (later the University of Windsor) and became first Black Canadian to hold a tenure-track position in a Canadian university. He was department head from 1974 to 1979. In 1967–68 he was president of the Canadian Association of University Teachers. He founded the Canadian College of Microbiologists in 1976, and served as its president until 1980.

All through this time, Howard was active in the civil rights battle. In Michigan, he was president of the National Association for the Advancement of Colored People (NAACP) and the founder of the local chapter. In 1962, he founded the Guardian Club, a civil rights organization, to fight racial discrimination in Windsor. In 1969, he was a founder and first President of the National Black Coalition of Canada. He was active in the New Democratic Party throughout the 1960s, and in 1984 he was elected as the NDP MP for the riding of Windsor Walkerville. He was a candidate for the party leadership in the 1989 leadership convention but lost to Audrey McLaughlin. Throughout his career, McCurdy was there to stand up for Black people and all of the oppressed minorities in the country.

Another prominent New Democrat in the period was Rosemary Brown, a Jamaican who had moved to Canada in 1950 to study at McGill. In 1972, she became the first Black woman elected to public office in Canada, serving in the B.C. Legislature as the NDP MLA for Vancouver-Burrard until 1986. In 1975, she came second to Ed Broadbent in the federal NDP leadership race. After fourteen years of service as an MLA, Rosemary would go on to serve as chief commissioner of the Ontario Human Rights Commission.

It wasn't until the 1990s that a Black woman was elected to the House of Commons. It was my friend Jean Augustine. She was politically active with the provincial Liberal Party and was appointed chair of the Metro Toronto Housing Authority in 1985. She ran in the federal election in 1993 and was elected by a wide margin and went on to serve as Prime Minister Chrétien's parliamentary secretary, and then Minister of State for Multiculturalism and the Status of Women.

Also prominent at the time was Zanana Akande, elected as a New Democratic MPP in the Rae government in 1990, becoming the first Black woman in the Ontario legislature. She resigned on August 31, 1994, in protest against Rae's handling of the Carlton Masters controversy. Masters, of Jamaican origin, was forced to resign as Ontario's agent general to the U.S. when he was accused of sexually harassing employees at his New York and Boston offices. Zanana made no bones about being disillusioned with party politics in Canada — not an unusual feeling among Black politicians. Some did well by avoiding the race issue as much as possible, but those who stood up to fight for their community against Canadian racism found a much chillier reception.

Some of the most important work on our behalf during this period was not done by the mainstream politicians, but by the activists at the ground level, especially those fighting to overcome the problems in Toronto's rapidly expanding high-rise immigrant ghetto in the Jane-Finch area where now more than 80% of the population was visible minorities. The first Jane-Finch community groups began to appear in the early 1970s, and by the end of the decade more than thirty grassroots organizations were fighting for the safety and dignity of their community.

The task was a large one. Black Creek, the neighbourhood at the heart of the Jane-Finch sector, was identified by the Toronto Summit Alliance's task force as one of the neighbourhoods in the city that had completely inadequate social services. The basic numbers tell it all. In North York during this period, the population of higher income families increased by 9% but the number of poor grew by 80.5%. Black Creek had the highest rate of racialized groups, immigrants, recent newcomers, children, youth, lone parents, low income families, low income unattached individuals, lowest median household income, higher unemployment, lower percentage of population with university education, and higher percentage of population with less than high school education.

In the face of such challenges, it was a struggle for both the political class and the grassroots organizers to keep a lid on things while Black youth faced, at every turn, harassment and rejection as doors leading to economic opportunities and decent jobs were closed to them.

I found it was impossible to sit around and do nothing.

Shortly after the launch of the Black Business and Professional Association, my friend Al Hamilton came to me to tell me that his newspaper, *Contrast*, was going under.

I told him not to let it go. I would step in as owner and publisher. We could not afford to lose our voice. We could not afford to lose any more of anything — it was time to build our own institutions and our own lives despite the too often hostile surroundings we had found ourselves in.

CHAPTER ELEVEN
BUSINESSMAN, PUBLISHER, ACTIVIST

Home, during this period, was not a refuge. My marriage was on the rocks and it was a painful time for both Carol and me. But even while our own relationship was coming apart, we understood that our relationships with our children had to remain strong. Even in the most difficult periods, we knew that we had produced three remarkable human beings together, and we had to continue to act as parents.

My children were and remain a great source of pride. From the beginning I found myself admiring them for their grit and persistence. Nicole was growing into an amazing young woman. She had attended Montessori school in the primary grades and was just entering Havergal College, a private girls' school. She would study there for several years before finishing at the public Leaside High School. She would go on to attend McGill, then the Sorbonne (mainly, I think, to be able to spend a year in Paris), and finished at the London School of Economics, where she received her master's.

The boys went through special education courses at the Arrowsmith School in Yorkville and demonstrated an ingrained love of sports, especially hockey. At the end of the 1980s, when they were in their late teens, they came to work for me at the nursing home. When they were old enough to move out on their own, we found a place for them in the home of a retired Jamaican woman, a registered nurse. The boys lived with her for many years while remaining an important part of my life, as they are today.

My life outside the home was busier than ever. When Al Hamilton said that he was ready to give up on *Contrast* for financial reasons, we sat down together to look at what could be done. Al was always dressed to the nines, always smoking, generally a pipe, and people noticed when he entered a room. He spoke forcefully and passionately, and he was fearless in calling out racism and injustice in Toronto, in Canada, and around the world. He was a fighter, and he practised a kind of pugilistic journalism that made even some members of the Black community describe the paper as "too Black." He didn't care. Before I met him in person, I knew Al Hamilton the fighter through the pages of *Contrast*, and I liked him from the beginning.

What Al was not, however, was a businessman. A playwright and a performer as well as a journalist, he too often showed the artist's disinterest for the bottom line.

The front page of a 1984 edition of Contrast.

Finally, he enlisted me to come in as publisher and provide the business sense as well as some new capital to invest in the paper. Al and I already knew we could work together. We had been founding members of the Committee for Due

Process, and he had been one of the first people I had called when I was launching the BBPA. He, in turn, had made *Contrast* a major sponsor of the Harry Jerome Awards, so we had already developed a good working relationship.

When I took over *Contrast* in April, 1983, I gave it a major overhaul that began with a bold black, yellow, and red sign outside its new storefront office on Bathurst Street just north of Bloor. By this time, Toronto's Black population had increased to 300,000, and the paper had a readership of 30,000 and a subscriptions base of 12,000. I increased the size of the paper from sixteen to twenty-four pages to try to make its content relevant to more people and then invested $50,000 in computerized typesetting equipment.

It was a special time to be publisher of *Contrast*, which in those days was at the heart of the Black community geographically as well as philosophically. Almost twenty years later, Royson James captured the essence of the period and the neighbourhood in his *Toronto Star* column:

> Emerging from the subway at Bathurst . . . this was once Grand Central Station for the black immigrant community. The cops camped out there — such was the perceived danger of the multitude of black kids pouring out of Central Technical School, bubbling, shouting, ghetto blasting with teenage abandonment . . .
>
> Bathurst St. was the axis of immigrant Caribbean-Canadian life. Honest Ed's was the black Eaton's. Go north past the subway to patty shops, barber shop, beauty shop. Go south from Honest Ed's and you pass

Ram's Roti, then Lennox St. Turn right to number
28, *Contrast Newspaper*, the "eyes, ears and voice of
Canada's black Community." . . .

At a time when black folks were dismissed as
a bloody nuisance and troublemakers not worthy
of Canadian citizenship, *Contrast* was a bulwark, a
shelter against a storm of media criticism and unfair
caricature and representation.

I was working with the eyes and ears and voice of the
Black community from my *Contrast* office in the morning,
then heading off to Mississauga to oversee the nursing
home business, where there were also daily emergencies to
deal with.

Time was, in fact, at a premium. *Contrast* needed a lot
of time as well as effort. Al had stayed on with the paper
as manager and sales manager, and he was supposed to be
bringing in ad revenues. But we discovered that many of
the businesses that advertised with us simply tossed our bills
to the back of their pile and never paid. And Al, no longer
financially responsible for the paper, seemed to expend
less energy booking ads. Even though our circulation was
increasing and we were getting great feedback on the paper's
improvements, it was a struggle to keep it going.

I have to say that, despite the challenges, from an
editorial point of view I am proud of the paper we published.
Ours was among the best coverage in Canada of the U.S.
invasion of Grenada and the disastrous implications it had
for the sovereign rights of all of the island countries in the
Caribbean. It was a natural story for us because we had

already been covering the Grenada revolutionary experiment and the darkening clouds over the island with the arrival of the Reagan administration in Washington. There was a great deal of support in Toronto for Maurice Bishop, the socialist prime minister of Grenada. Jean Augustine, then principal of St. Felix Senior Elementary School, was the head of the Canada Grenadian society, so there was real concern in the Toronto West Indian community when the revolution began spiralling out of control and the Americans sent in the marines with the backing of Jamaican Prime Minister Edward Seaga.

We also kept a close eye on race relations in the city while at the same time broadening our appeal with Black-oriented lifestyle pieces. Our sports section had the same unique mix, featuring NHL scores and articles on the hapless Maple Leafs, with coverage of cricket tournaments in the West Indies and special features on the Black football greats playing for the Toronto Argonauts.

An issue that always received major play in the paper was the struggle against the apartheid regime in South Africa. It was one that we hammered home in almost every edition in boycott reports, editorials, and even editorial cartoons. A typical one showed a guy and his wife sitting with the newspaper over coffee, reading a story about the Ontario ombudsman invited to South Africa to speak about setting up an ombudsman system there.

"It says South Africa wants an ombudsman just like ours," the guy tells his wife.

"Yes," she replies, "one who doesn't mind associating with racists."

That summed up our direct approach on the issue, and I admit that in my personal life I was even more direct. I sent monthly cheques to the African National Congress (ANC) office in Zambia, and I am not ashamed to say that on more than one occasion I found myself accidentally knocking over South African wine displays at the liquor store. That is how deeply I felt about the outrages committed daily against the people of South Africa.

Al and I even addressed this issue with the leader of the Ontario Progressive Conservative Party, Larry Grossman, a Forest Hill Collegiate alumnus. We managed to get a meeting with him as representatives of *Contrast*, and we demanded that Ontario stop selling South African wines in government stores. Grossman seemed sympathetic, but this was always the Canadian politicians' response. Sympathetic sounds until you left their office. Then you and your issues were quickly forgotten.

Contrast did not forget, though. The boycott remained front and centre on our pages, as did the demand to free ANC president Nelson Mandela. In the late 1980s, I and others from *Contrast* even picketed our own Harry Jerome Awards dinner against Prime Minister Mulroney's attendance as a way to bring attention to his government's continuing complicity with South Africa.

Our offices became a centre for this fight and for Black community resistance. Local visiting civil rights activists stopped by to touch base and to meet others. The paper also served as a launch pad for many young journalists who went on to build international reputations, including music journalist Curtis Bailey, known for his encyclopedic knowledge of jazz; Olivia Grange-Walker, who went on to become the minister of culture, youth, and sports in Jamaica; Jojo Chintoh, who worked with Citytv; future *Toronto Star* columnist Royson James; Harold Hoyte, who went on to publish the *Nation* newspaper in Barbados; even the singer-songwriter-composer and cultural historian Tiki Mercury-Clarke; and local legends like Norman "Otis" Richmond, the CKLN DJ and music journalist. Cecil Foster left for the *Star*, then the book world; Arnold Auguste founded rival *Share* newspaper; Tom Godfrey went to the *Toronto Sun*. Another contributor, Austin Clarke, was well known and highly respected before he began writing for *Contrast*, and we were delighted to have him grace our pages.

For me it was a strange life, spending half the day in this atmosphere of resistance then rushing off to the nursing home to work at making the money that I was slowly, and then with increasing speed, losing at *Contrast*.

The nursing home also had its challenges. With a staff that grew to 150, personnel issues took up a great deal of time. Finding enough replacement staff was always difficult, especially for weekends and holidays, and to make up for it we recruited a hundred volunteers who could spend time with the patients and free up staff for other work. In return, we spent a lot of effort showing our appreciation to the volunteers, as well as to the staff. I tried as much as possible to keep the relations on the human level. We would have monthly staff birthday luncheons with a monetary gift for those with birthdays that month. As an added inducement, we had five-, ten-, fifteen-, and twenty-five-year recognition awards, again with a monetary component. Depending on their financial circumstances, I even provided interest-free student loans for the schooling of children of staff members and subsidized airline tickets for funeral travel. These measures worked because employees understood that they were respected as people and colleagues with full lives outside of work and were not just cogs in the machine. They earned me the loyalty and dedication of many key staff members who stuck with me over forty years.

Less easy to handle were the complaints from our patients' relatives. Part of the issue, it seemed, was that a significant number of them felt guilty for not caring for their loved ones themselves in their own homes and overcompensated by hovering around and picking fights with the residence staff. To give the family members a window into the operation of the residence, and to let them air their grievances and even participate in the discussion over food with the dietary staff, we set up a relative support group.

The most difficult issue of all, and the one I really hated to deal with, was allegations of patient abuse. These were often difficult to prove either way, and we received very little outside help in resolving them. In fact, once when I fired a worker for hitting a patient, I was forced by the Labour Board to reinstate her. My only recourse was to remind the staff time and again that quite possibly they too would be elderly one day, and they should treat the residents with understanding and the respect they deserved.

Fortunately, the abuse incidents were very rare and overall we had a good reputation in the community in the areas of staff training, patient care, and staff relations. On most days, it was a pleasure to arrive in the complex, which was beautifully landscaped with Little Etobicoke Creek winding through the property. Senior staff were like family and we shared whatever burdens arose during the day.

The most prickly people I dealt with at the nursing home turned out to be two Mississauga mayors: a former mayor and the current one.

The first was Dr. Martin Dobkin, my medical director. He had been elected the youngest mayor in Mississauga history in 1973, but he lost the 1976 election. Shortly afterwards he showed up at my door asking for the job, with a very sizeable retainer.

Because he had been mayor, he had some inside knowledge of upcoming developments and asked me to come in on some deals — mainly as the guy who capitalized them. It was an odd situation, and many things about it made me uncomfortable, but Dr. Dobkin was with me for eight years. We parted over an incident involving my mother. I had brought her to Canada to have her cataracts removed, and she had the operation at Sunnybrook. When she was recovering at home, she needed eye drops and I was in a hurry and asked Dobkin if he could write a prescription.

"I'm not the doctor for your whole family," he said. And he refused.

I found his attitude more than a little insulting — it was for eye drops for my mother, not for some illicit opiate. I pointed out he had done very well working for me. He shrugged that off by saying they were his patients. I reminded him that they were in my nursing home, and our dispute ended with Dr. Dobkin no longer in my employ.

As it turned out, I wasn't a big fan of his main successor as mayor either. Hazel McCallion was elected Mississauga mayor in 1978 and stayed in office until 2014 — a total of thirty-six years. My dealings with her were always, to put it nicely, odd. In one incident, the city had approved development of a piece of land upstream from me on the old creek bed, and we were hit by ongoing flooding. I dealt with the city environment people, and they seemed to be understanding, but then I went to see Hazel at her office with my lawyer, Eddie Goodman, who also happened to be chair of the Ontario Progressive Conservatives and one of the builders of the Big Blue Machine. Hazel was late arriving for our meeting. When she finally breezed in, she was talking a mile a minute about how it was all just politics. She kept repeating it and, to be honest, not making a lot of sense. We left midway through the harangue without any help at all from the mayor.

My second encounter was even more bizarre. I was in a dispute with the gas company that I had dealt with for twenty years but which suddenly instituted a policy of requiring a $25,000 deposit for commercial users. I had always paid my bill on time and thought this cash grab was ridiculous. I refused to pay. So the company just went ahead and added it directly to my monthly bill. I still refused to pay, and they threatened to cut off gas to the nursing home, in the middle of winter, and freeze the 200 seniors there.

As a fairly important Mississauga institution and employer of 150 people, I called the mayor for help in the dispute and left her a message.

Weeks later, I received a call that went something like this.

"I hear you haven't been paying your bills."

"I have been paying my bills," I said. "It is just that —"

"You have to pay your bills," she interrupted. "Everyone has to pay their bills! It is like if you don't pay your taxes, we will take away your house."

"I have been paying my taxes . . ."

"You have to pay your bills. We have all these problems with these grow-ops growing marijuana . . ."

It seemed now that Hazel was free-associating. Jamaican Black, energy bills, must be grow-op.

"I didn't call you to talk about grow-ops," I said.

"They are all over. Grow-ops everywhere. We —"

I quietly replaced the receiver. I don't know how long she ranted about grow-ops before she finally realized she was talking to herself, but I didn't have time for people like Hazel in those days. And I still don't.

When I finished dealing with the nursing home challenges, I would return to the mountain of challenges I had to deal with at *Contrast*. It all began to unravel after three years when we prepared a Christmas edition. Al and I had discussed a major push to increase holiday ad revenues to keep us going into the new year.

When we were ready to do the final layout, I checked with Al about our ad revenues for the edition. Not only was there no push, there was a significant and inexplicable drop.

I confronted him. He was evasive. I still don't know what

was going on but, from my point of view, it meant I had to close the paper. Al wanted me to simply give it back to him, and part of me wondered later if that hadn't been his plan in those final months: let the paper starve from revenues so that I would return it to him. Whatever the motivation, I knew that *Contrast* had really gone under because we tried to make a professional paper at a time when our community wasn't able to fully support it. Al didn't have the resources to keep it going and in the end I sold it to Horace Gooden, another Jamaican-born businessman who pledged to try "to save the paper for the community." Within a year, he closed it down for a reorganization. The paper would return for several more years, but it was never the same and, finally, other smaller papers would fill the gap. The most successful was *Share*, a giveaway paper started by former *Contrast* reporter Arnold Auguste that began in the 1970s as a kind of bland good-news-bearer but matured into the very balanced and respectable newspaper it remains today.

Thankfully, our *Contrast* failure didn't sour my friendship with Al. We would remain in the fight together until the end, which in Al's case came far too soon. He died at the age of only sixty-six in 1994, and his loss was felt throughout the community.

At the end of the 1980s, we were still working together. And our solidarity and the solidarity of all of Black Toronto was more necessary than ever. The situation of Blacks in Toronto was not improving — in fact, it had gotten worse since the beginning of the decade. And once again, the measure was provided by another, this time much longer, spree of police killings and public abuse of Black citizens. The first casualty was Lester Donaldson, and he became another high profile symbol of police brutality against Blacks in Toronto.

The government had made only the most tepid response to the mobilizations against the earlier Evans and Johnson killings by enacting, in 1981, the Office of the Public Complaints Commissioner (OPCC) where civilians could report incidents of police brutality. But the OPCC was still biased in favour of police and offered no community control of the complaints process. Nothing had really changed by 1988 when Lester Donaldson was gunned down.

Lester Donaldson was born in Jamaica in 1943, moved to England at the age of sixteen, and came to Canada in 1968, when he was twenty-five years old. He returned to Jamaica for a few years but came back to Canada in 1977. By this time it was clear that there was something not right with him. He complained of hearing voices and thought that there was a transmitter inside his head. In 1978, Donaldson was diagnosed by a psychiatrist as a paranoid schizophrenic. In 1981, he was charged with minor drug offences and put on probation. In 1982, he was charged with more minor drug offences and served sixty days in jail on weekends. Things were more serious in the spring of 1988 when Lester was suspected of a break and enter and, during a chase with police officers, he tried to fight off the officers with a shovel. He was shot in the thigh by the police and charged with breaking and entering and assault with a weapon. The shooting by police left him with a permanent limp.

On August 7, 1988, police went to the building where Lester Donaldson lived after receiving complaints that someone was tampering with fuse boxes, cutting wires, and playing with lights. Lester was suspected, but the police had no contact with him that evening. Two days later, another complaint brought police officers to Lester's place at 192 Lauder Avenue. The address was recognized from the earlier incident. A total of five officers entered Lester's room and stayed for twenty minutes.

Lester was obviously a troubled individual, and what he needed was emergency mental health intervention much more than policing. But the police refused to call for professional help. After talking with him for those twenty minutes, they moved to arrest him. Lester, they claimed, produced a small paring knife, and a confrontation took place. Lester was fatally shot by one of the officers, Constable Deviney, from a distance of four feet.

The first indication that something was very wrong with this killing were the falsehoods the police began to tell. In their first press advisory on the killing, the police said that when they responded to that call, Donaldson was holding people hostage in his rooming house. But Donaldson, it quickly became clear, was shot dead while he was alone with the police in his apartment. A subsequent inquest uncovered a whole series of police fabrications around the incident.

On Saturday, August 13, a group of us, many of whom had been involved years earlier in the Committee for Due Process and the Dudley Laws' Albert Johnson Defence Committee Against Police Brutality, called for a demonstration in front of Constable Deviney's thirteenth-division headquarters. Very quickly the crowd swelled to more than a thousand people demanding that charges be laid against the officer who pulled the trigger.

After the demonstration, a number of us, including Charlie Roach and Jean Augustine, who were also at the march, went to a meeting called by Dudley Laws to launch a new organization, the Black Action Defence Committee (BADC), to fight against this sort of police killing. In the press, I was named with fifteen others as part of the founding group, but in this case the moving force really was Dudley Laws.

Dudley was someone I always admired. He was a fellow Jamaican, and we were more or less the same age. But when Dudley was twenty-one years old he went to London, where he instantly became involved in the struggle for justice. He came to Canada in 1965, and he joined the Jamaican Canadian Association in 1967 and UNIA in 1968, becoming president of the organization in 1972 and later serving as UNIA's executive director. Over the years, Dudley would become our social, moral, and legal compass. Instantly recognizable for his black beret, he was a fearless Garvey-ite. He was never afraid to speak truth to power, no matter what the consequences. In his case, the consequences would be considerable when he was set upon by the Toronto Police Department in an unprecedented police attack on a civilian.

The BADC had a much broader anti-racist vision than merely defending against police killings, but these killings were happening with an alarming frequency, keeping the organization and its activists busy for the next several years.

To illustrate the scope of the disaster, I will list shootings and other humiliations at the hands of Toronto and some other Canadian police forces during the late 1980s and through the 1990s. You can understand how, in a very real way, Blacks in Toronto were feeling hunted.

On December 8, 1988, a few months after the Donaldson killing, seventeen-year-old Michael Wade Lawson of Mississauga was shot in the back of the head while joyriding in a stolen car.

Ten months later, police shot twenty-three-year-old Sophia Cook of Brampton when she was strapped into the passenger seat of a car. That car, too, was stolen, but that is not a firing squad offence, and Sophia had no connection whatsoever with the theft — after missing her bus, she had accepted a ride in the car.

Six months later, at Montreal's Thunderdome nightclub, twenty-six-year-old Leslie Presley was shot numerous times.

A month later, in May 1990, an unarmed sixteen-year-old named Marlon Neal fled a police radar trap in Scarborough and was shot.

Just over a year later, in Montreal, on July 3, 1991, a SWAT team sergeant shot twenty-four-year-old Marcellus Francois in the head. The police claimed that it was a case of mistaken identity.

On November 9, 1991, twenty-four-year-old Jonathan Howell, a Toronto resident, was permanently brain-damaged when Constable Carl Sokolowski shot him. In a judge-only trial (no jury), Sokolowski was found guilty of careless use of a firearm but was given an absolute discharge.

Less than a month later, twenty-one-year-old Royan

Bagnaut was shot in the arm and chest after he allegedly stole a purse while armed with a knife. The shooter, Constable Douglas Lines, said he'd thought Royan had a gun. No gun was found.

On May 2, 1992, twenty-two-year-old Raymond Lawrence was shot and killed by undercover cop, Robert Rice, after a long foot chase.

On January 1, 1993, practising Rastafarian Trevor Kelly of Montreal was fatally shot in the back. According to the Sûreté du Québec investigation, Trevor's killer was justified in his actions. Officer Richard Massé claimed that he had believed his partner's life was in danger because Trevor was standing over him with a paring knife. Investigators reportedly found a kitchen knife near Kelly's body; no fingerprints were on it.

On April 20, 1993, twenty-one-year-old Ian Clifford Coley was shot twice in the chest by Constable Rick Shank in Scarborough. The shooting was fatal.

On September 29, 1994, Torontonian Albert Moses, 41, was in his room when police officer Jeffrey Vance shot him in the face. Vance alleged that Moses had assaulted his partner with a hammer.

On January 10, 1996, in downtown Toronto, Sergeant Benedetto Troina fired four bullets into the chest of Tommy Anthony Barnett, age twenty-two, who the police claimed was unsheathing a sword.

Two months later, in the Jane-Finch area, Constable Andy Kis shot Andrew Bramwell, age twenty-four, to death. Investigators recovered a Glock pistol from the scene; it had not been fired. The Special Investigations

Unit cleared Kis of criminal wrongdoing.

On June 11, 1996, two officers shot to death twenty-four-year-old Wayne Rick Williams, a student at Seneca College who was suffering from depression and schizophrenia. Four bullets struck his body; the police claimed that he had a knife in his hand in the driveway of his home at the time of the shooting. One of the shooters, Kenneth Harrison, had been involved in a previous fatal shooting.

On March 30, 1997, Rick Shank — the same officer who had killed Ian Clifford Coley four years earlier — fatally shot unarmed thirty-one-year-old Hugh Dawson while he was sitting, strapped in, at the steering wheel of his car. Shank struck Hugh with nine shots; in court, firearm examiner Michael Clarke said that the "muzzle of the pistol was about one to three inches from Dawson when it was fired, leaving powder burns on his clothing." The police said Hugh had grabbed two officers' guns, but his fingerprints were never found on the weapons.

And finally, on one of the last events of the millennium, on December 31, 1999, Henry Musaka, age twenty-six, was killed by two shots to the head and one to the chest. Police had been called to St. Michael's Hospital, where Henry was holding an ER doctor hostage. Henry had gone to the hospital with his son, who was having trouble breathing. Hospital staff told him no pediatrician was available, and he would have to wait an hour to see a doctor. Any Black parent will understand how this dangerous indifference affected Henry, finally prompting his desperate, foolish, and ultimately fatal action. Afterwards, the police found an unloaded pellet gun in his possession.

Even this barrage of police killings of Blacks was only part of the story. There were countless other examples of public abuse. One that sticks in my mind, because it was so outrageous, is the abuse of a Jamaican tourist, Audrey Smith, a thirty-seven-year-old public sector worker and mother of five who, in the summer of 1993, was accused of possessing drugs, detained in a police cruiser, and finally strip-searched, completely naked, in a busy street in downtown Toronto's Parkdale neighbourhood. The police found no drugs. The officers responsible for what was arguably a sexual assault were not even disciplined.

This had become the rule rather than the exception. A *Toronto Star* report has pointed out that of the nine police charged in the killings through the '80s and '90s, only one was convicted, and he received an absolute discharge. The other eight had the charges dismissed or withdrawn, or were found to be not guilty even though an internal police investigation found that some officers had been habitually using racist slurs.

These inevitable acquittals only made the problem worse. For example, after much protest, Lester Donaldson's killer, Constable Deviney, was finally charged with manslaughter on January 11, 1989, but he was acquitted less than two years later, causing another round of indignation.

This became a familiar pattern for the BADC. We demonstrated after each of these incidents of killings or public humiliations of members of our community. Then we demonstrated again when the police were acquitted or otherwise exonerated by a corrupt system. This meant a lot of marching on our part, but it was really all we had to let the larger Canadian society know that these abuses would never be accepted. During the demonstrations, I used my station wagon as an on-site ambulance for anyone who needed help during the march, with first aid supplies taken from the nursing home. When possible, I was accompanied by a Haitian doctor friend. We were absolutely determined to protest the outrages against us.

The police treated us like enemy aliens. This became blatantly clear in 1989, when it was revealed one of Toronto's few Black officers, Denny Dias, had been carrying out undercover surveillance of thirteen activist and civil rights organizations and eighteen Black individuals. His unit spied on the National Council of Jamaicans, the Coalition of Visible Minority Women, the Justice for Wade Lawson Committee, and the National Black Coalition of Canada, as well Dudley Laws, Ras Rico I, Dari Meade, Dr. Wilson Head, Kamala-Jean Gopie, Evelyn Lennon-Lyon (mother of Michael Wade Lawson, the Mississauga teen slain by police), and Greg Bobb. None of these individuals had criminal convictions.

Their main target was clearly Dudley Laws and the Black Action Defence Committee. Dudley didn't pull punches, and after the unprecedented spree of police killings of Blacks, some of which seemed like murders to us, Dudley called the Metro Toronto Police "the most brutal and murderous in North America." They were determined to punish him for his defiance.

The fact that one of the few Black police officers on the force was used to spy on other Blacks was also a sad testament to the state of race relations on the force at this time. In later years, a number of high-quality officers would rise through the ranks — like Keith Forde, who in 1972 was only the eighteenth Black officer to be hired in the whole history of Toronto, and who went on to become the city's deputy chief.

But in 1991, the police were clearly obsessed with nailing the hides of uppity Blacks to the wall and a chief target was Dudley Laws. The Police Association attack began with a campaign to silence Roy Williams, a political moderate on the Police Services Board who had defended Dudley Laws' freedom to express opinions on the police; Williams had also raised the association's ire by encouraging the community to donate to Laws' defence fund. Then the association went after Dudley directly, with the Metro Toronto Police Association launching a multi-million-dollar defamation lawsuit against him.

In October 1991, Dudley Laws was the victim of an immigration entrapment scheme concocted by the Toronto Police, RCMP, and U.S. border police that led to charges for smuggling immigrants. These were withdrawn in October 1998 on the condition that Dudley perform 200 hours of community service and maintain "no record of criminal charges" for a year. Reportedly, the investigation of Dudley cost between $400,000 and $1,000,000 and employed thirty-six police officers — at one point they rented a loft across the street from his office so they could keep an eye on him twenty-four hours a day.

Because of the endless police killings of mainly young Blacks, the outright persecution of Dudley Laws for speaking up, and the revelations that virtually anyone in the Black community who offered resistance was under aggressive state surveillance, a truly poisonous atmosphere prevailed in Toronto in the late 1980s and well into the 1990s.

One expression of the profound alienation of our people was the so-called Yonge Street Riot in 1992, another demonstration sparked by a police shooting. This time the victim was a twenty-two-year-old Black kid, Raymond Lawrence, who was fleeing police on foot on May 2, 1992. The policeman who shot and killed him, Constable Robert Rice, said that Lawrence had stopped and turned around and threatened him with a knife. A knife was found near Lawrence's lifeless body, but his fingerprints were not on it. Rice was never charged and he was quietly exonerated by the Special Investigations Unit after a cursory four-week investigation.

The Lawrence shooting came only weeks after the two police officers charged with manslaughter and aggravated assault for shooting seventeen-year-old Michael Wade Lawson were acquitted of all charges by an all-white jury.

On May 4, the Black Action Defence Committee amassed on Yonge Street just south of Bloor to protest the killing of Lawrence, the Lawson verdict, and the intense and ongoing police harassment of Toronto's Black communities, and to stand in solidarity with the ongoing Rodney King uprising in Los Angeles, which had followed the acquittal of the police officers filmed mercilessly beating King on an L.A. street. BADC began the march to the U.S. Consulate on University Avenue to underline to Canadians that you could find the same brutality against Blacks in Canada that we had seen in the U.S.

It was a small demonstration to start with, about sixty people; but as they began to march, the numbers grew with participants chanting "no justice, no peace!" as they moved toward Nathan Phillips Square. After speeches at city hall denouncing the police, the march doubled back on Yonge, heading northwards. BADC leadership drew the formal demonstration to a close, concluding with a singing of "Lift Every Voice and Sing."

But this time, the crowd didn't disperse.

As the protesters moved up Yonge Street, windows were smashed and police attempts to intervene were met by a hail of stones and bottles.

The police attempted to block the march at Bloor, parking two buses across the road. But the crowd surged toward the roadblock and the police moved the buses and retreated along Bloor West. The demonstrators followed them to the police station where a pitched battle ensued that was only broken up by police on horseback arriving cavalry-style, wielding batons to beat back the protesters. In the end, more than thirty people were arrested and many were injured, including some of the police.

While BADC had ended its participation in the protest before the vandalism began, it did not disavow it or the people participating in it. That night, during an emergency meeting at Dudley's office while the broken glass still littered Yonge Street, we decided that this position was the only honourable one. We knew that the police would try to use this incident to crack down on Black youth and their defenders but we would not fall into the trap of equating some broken glass with the relentless gunning down of our people. At the press conference the morning after, Dudley Laws said: "What we saw yesterday was the frustration and the anger of the people coming out. We have waited for the justice system to deal justly with our community and it has failed."

The media called this the "Yonge Street Riot" but one of the BADC founders more accurately described it as the "Yonge Street Rebellion." In a sense, the Ontario government understood it that way, too, because in the wake of this rebellion they appointed Stephen Lewis to report on the state of race relations in the province.

Lewis would bring the first real moment of frankness to the discussion of race relations in Canada. In his findings he stated, "what we are dealing with, at root, and fundamentally, is anti-Black racism. . . . It is Blacks who are being shot, it is Black youth that are unemployed in excessive numbers, it is Black students who are being inappropriately streamed in schools, it is Black kids who are disproportionately dropping out, it is housing communities with large concentrations of Black residents where the sense of vulnerability and disadvantage is most acute, it is Black employees, professional and non-professional, on whom the doors of upward equity slam shut. Just as the soothing balm of 'multiculturalism' cannot mask racism, so racism cannot mask its primary target."

These words were encouraging to hear: only when Canadians faced the problem would we have hope of properly addressing it. Unfortunately, this sort of frankness about Canadian racism was rare during a period when the situation was steadily worsening. What we needed as a community was our own voice. One that would speak loud and clear, and most importantly would speak to our young. Our newspaper, *Contrast*, was only partially successful in this, and unfortunately it wasn't financially sustainable. By the time Al and I were putting the paper to bed for the last time, we were already looking at a bigger project. We began to look for a loud voice for our community on Toronto's airwaves, and this would consume us for the next decade and more.

CHAPTER TWELVE

LOSING LOVED ONES
AND LOSING A BATTLE

In the mid-1980s I was just entering my fifties. My life in Toronto was already busy with business interests and community commitments. But I had another obligation: looking after my mother. She was getting old and her health was failing. I visited her in Jamaica whenever I could and she also came to visit me in Canada, sometimes because she needed medical care in Toronto.

She had no real pension, so I was taking care of her expenses, including her medical costs. I know she felt uneasy about this — she was a proudly independent woman who had been taking care of herself since my father's death in 1963 — but she needed help. To repay some of this help, she insisted I take over what was left of the family land in Industry Cove; after she was gone, I could sell it to recoup a part of the money I'd spent taking care of her. From my point of view, this offer was completely unnecessary — but I knew it was important for her. She wanted to feel that she was paying her own way.

In my trips back to Jamaica, I was no more encouraged by prospects there than I had been in the 1950s when I left. If anything, things had gotten worse. The 1980s in Jamaica was the decade of Edward Seaga and the Jamaica Labour Party. Seaga, a U.S.-born, Harvard-educated anthropologist who made his mark as a record producer, had swept into power in October 1980 after the tumultuous decade in which Michael Manley's path of democratic socialism was suppressed by behind-the-scenes CIA maneuvers and by open hostility from the U.S. State Department and U.S.-controlled international financial institutions.

The 1980 election campaign felt more like a coup than a peaceful transition of power. Edward Seaga received early help from the IMF, which enacted such harsh measures against Jamaica in the spring of 1980 that Manley was forced to pull out of his agreement with it. From then on, the economy went into a tailspin, and the gunfire in the streets during the fall campaign finished the job. Seaga won in a landslide, and one of his first acts before instituting his neo-liberal program was to satisfy the incoming Reagan administration in Washington by expelling Ulises Estrada, the Cuban Ambassador to Jamaica, and severing diplomatic ties with Cuba. Seaga remained in power until 1989 with his permanent austerity program for the island, which further strangled the economy to the point where some Jamaicans joked that, between them, Manley and Seaga had managed to discredit the two leading economic theories of our time: socialism and capitalism.

By 1989, when a newly chastised Manley was re-elected, he and Jamaica as a whole appeared to accept its fate as an economically stagnant island firmly in the American orbit. The economy would henceforth focus on tourism and foreign aid. Manley's most notable initiative during this mandate was increasing food stamps for the poor. Jamaica would no longer be a place for big dreams.

For me, the decade of the 1990s began with what would turn out to be my most difficult year, personally and professionally.

On the personal side, I lost two of the people I was closest to, not only in the same year but within eleven days of each other in February 1990: my mother and my second mother, Violet Blackman.

My mother passed away on February 11, 1990, after a long illness. As it happened, it was the day Nelson Mandela was released from prison, and that news came to me first. The day started out with euphoria: Mandela, finally a free man, was promising the massive crowds gathered to witness his release that, after twenty-seven years in prison, he was still loyal to the ANC goals, and he was still ready to die in the fight to end apartheid. His release and his unique combination of humility and strength touched the world.

"I stand here before you not as a prophet but as a humble servant of you, the people," he said. "Your tireless and heroic sacrifices have made it possible for me to be here today. I therefore place the remaining years of my life in your hands. Our march to freedom is irreversible. We must not allow fear to stand in our way."

After hearing his speech, I called my sister Barbara in Montego Bay to ask how our mother, still almost universally known as "Miss Ina," was doing. Her health had recently taken a downward dip, and I was in regular touch with Barbara about her progress. My sister's housekeeper answered the phone. I asked where Barbara was, and she said that she had left in a rush for the hospital. They had called, the housekeeper said, and told my sister that "Miss Ina" was dying.

That was how I found out. With a heavy heart, I called around to my sisters and brothers and we began planning the funeral. It was held at Lucea Anglican Church, less than a kilometre from Ruseas High School. My mother had lived most of her life in Hanover Parish, and because of the way she had lived it — serving as both a family court judge and justice of the peace — her passing was felt far and wide. I was asked to prepare a eulogy and I had trouble listing all the people I wanted to mention, from the local bishop, to clergy from across the island, to the high schools who were honouring her, to the local parishioners who took the time to decorate the church to mark her passing. It was of course an emotional time for our family, and it was difficult to find the words to express the love all of her children had for her and the pride we felt at how she had touched so many. I told the packed crowd that as her children we were at least thankful that she lived long enough for us to return the love and great affection she so willingly and joyfully gave to us.

I also thanked her for giving us an example of generosity

*At the Industry Cove Basic School in Jamaica that
my mother founded, which I still support.*

to follow — I mentioned the numerous children we had
around our dinner table when we were growing up, who she
raised as her own — and for teaching us the simple manners
that would allow us to converse with labourers or heads of

state. She wanted to ensure that no doors were closed to us, while stressing that we had a duty to give to those who were less fortunate. We loved her not only for the care and love she gave us, and the sacrifices she made for us, but for her example of how to live a life.

"How could we not feel proud," I asked, "of a mother who feeds the hungry, shelters the homeless, and as a justice of the peace was known as someone who made decisions on the basis of compassion and mercy." Her contribution to the Parish, which included founding and running the Industry Cove Basic School, a preschool for the local children, had been recognized by a prime ministerial award given to her by Edward Seaga. But her real legacy was in Industry Cove, with the many children other than her own whom she had cared for and helped raise. She was an inspiration not only to her family but to the whole community.

I was only back in Toronto a couple of days when I lost my second mother, Violet Blackman.

To many of us, Violet represented the living history of Blacks in Toronto. When she arrived in Canada in 1920, Blacks were, as she put it, "a novelty" in this highly controlled white city. The tiny, fragile community had gradually built itself up, surviving by creating its own parallel institutions, from Garvey's Universal Negro Improvement Association, which plugged the community into Black culture around the world, to Mike "Coffee" Williams' grocery store on Queen Street, which imported foods from the Caribbean that were unheard of in the beef-and-potatoes Canadian diet.

Fortunately, Violet also lived long enough to be honoured for her contribution. In 1985, she was given a Harry Jerome Award for her lifetime contribution to our community; and in 1989, she was made a member of the Order of Ontario "for services to humanity" in a batch of honourees that included John Bassett, Morley Callaghan, and Norman Jewison.

When interviewed about the Ontario award, Violet spoke mainly about her involvement in the Marcus Garvey movement and its focus on self-government and self-determination for Black people. She also spoke of her deep disappointment when the UNIA building was sold — it was more than just a building housing a cultural centre. To her it could have been a potential legacy for the young generation, a permanent landmark and a hall of fame where they could go and see names of accomplished Black people. "What have we got to show our children? That's what bothers me," she said.

Marcus Garvey's chair may be safely ensconced in the Jamaican Canadian Association office but a historical institute to Black Canada remains to be built. For now, what we have is Violet's legacy: all the young men and women, and their children, whom she helped build full and productive lives in unfriendly territory.

Throughout her life, Violet was a woman who emanated strength and intelligence. And a delightful stubbornness. I found this even at the end when I visited her in the hospital and learned that she had insisted that doctors making the rounds not bother her at certain hours when her favourite soap operas were on. That was pure Violet. Today, not only the Black Community but the whole society bears the imprint of her humanity. Her achievements in building Toronto's Black community have earned her the great respect and affection we all feel toward her.

Perhaps because of the example set by these two women, I was thinking more and more about our young people in Canada during this period, and I was worried about them. One incident that stuck in my mind was a news report of a violent battle between Black and white students at Cole Harbour High School in Nova Scotia, across the bay from Halifax. This incident began as a fight between two individuals, one Black and one white, but then escalated into a racial brawl. The police moved in to stop it, and, of course, the people they maced were Black students who weren't even involved in the fighting. Recalling my own unhappy years as a young Black man in Nova Scotia, and thinking of my mother and her profound faith in education, I arranged for two $7,000 scholarships for Cole Harbour students. In the wake of the race riot, the provincial government did enact some new measures in the form of anti-racist courses in the school, but the school has had further serious racial incidents in 2008 and again in 2009. There is no indication that things have really changed. But at least I was able to help a couple of students get out of the jam that history had placed them in, and I hope they will reach a point where they are able to return the favour to the next generation. Since then, I have become involved in giving scholarships where I can, for young people in Canada and also in Jamaica, often working with Conny Campbell and some other friends from Cornwall to give a leg up to the kids in need in Hanover Parish.

But of course scholarships cannot solve the enormous problem of Black youth growing up in a society that tells them in a thousand little ways that they are less than their fellow citizens. One of the solutions, I decided, was to create a large public space where they and their values were recognized and affirmed.

The idea of launching a Black radio station was in the air. While I was still publishing *Contrast*, I had written the CRTC to ask about the possibility of acquiring a licence for a Black station in the Toronto area the next time a frequency came up.

From then on, *Contrast* morphed into the radio station project. I heard that there was another group that was floating similar ideas, and finally a large group of twenty-five investors, mainly members of the Black Business and Professional Association, came together to form Milestone Communications Inc. and apply for the frequency 92.5 FM. We met all together for the first time in the Cassels Brock law office to set up a limited partnership that would allow us to begin to raise funds. It would be an expensive start-up because we had to open an office and hire a communication lawyer, a corporate lawyer, and researchers to see if the music we proposed had an audience, as well as an engineer to research the reach and contours of our broadcast pattern, a writer to write the application, and community workers to solicit letters of support for our application.

To no one's surprise, our research revealed an effective ban on playing Black music on Toronto's most popular stations. Most young Black Torontonians were listening to WBLK out of Buffalo in the same way that in the 1950s we had listened to Black music coming out of Detroit.

What we also found was that this exclusion was taking money out of the city, since Black night clubs in Toronto and other youth-oriented Black businesses were advertising on the Buffalo station because they knew their target market was listening to it. When word got out that our group was making the pitch for a Toronto station, we found natural alliances with Black musicians not only in Toronto but across Canada, where they felt similarly excluded from the airwaves.

Looking back, the CRTC application in 1990 for Canada's first Black radio station had an almost quixotic feel to it. We were more than two dozen stakeholders who were certain of our cause and expecting that the collection of political bureaucrats who run the CRTC would welcome us with open arms. With the legal fees and all of the other expenses, the bid would cost us $1.2 million out of our own pockets.

In our CRTC brief, we said we would build a station with a strong degree of loyalty from the Black community because of who we were and what we were offering. Blacks would listen to the station, we said, "not only from the standpoint of the format which will play all of their favourite music, but also from a sense of community commitment to a cause, to an ideal, to a concept that has been a long time coming." We could say this with confidence because of the amazing support we received from the community at every stage of our preparation.

By the time the hearings took place, many of us were thinking it was in the bag and already looking ahead to a victory celebration. But a conversation I had with one of our lawyers alerted me that not all the players were purely devoted to our Black radio bid as a noble cause: he told me that he liked taking the subway to work because he could include that time in his billable hours.

When we arrived at the hearings, it was also apparent that the CRTC was not quite ready for us. Their first question was, "Mr. Jolly, what is Black Music?"

This was in 1990. I answered that Black Music was what Black musicians made and Black people listened to, with, I think, some historical references to blues, jazz, Motown, and reggae, and to what was often called "dance music." But we were surprised at the question because it seemed to doubt the very validity of the genre we were proposing. In fact, from then on the commissioners tended to refer to our genre as "dance music" rather than "Black music."

An indication that the team we had assembled really didn't have experience in the arcane world of the CRTC came later during the hearings when the commission asked us to defend our revenue figures. Our expert was not present at that moment, and we could not immediately contact him. Our lawyer advised us that that was it, we would have to withdraw. I told him no way and approached the counsel for the CRTC to ask for time to produce the numbers, and she said, "Sure, no problem. You can bring it tomorrow."

These were only worrisome details at the time. But what was finally clear in the CRTC decision was that the political bureaucrats who run the CRTC had no desire to give the

Black community a radio licence, and they were prepared to handle it in the very Canadian way of accepting our application with a warm smile then tossing it in the trash can as we headed out the door.

That, finally, was what happened. At the outset, we were told that our bid put us near the top of the list. But after the week of hearings and three months of deliberations, the CRTC was happy to announce that the new frequency would be awarded to . . . Rawlco.

Rawlco? It was a bid for a country and western music station for Toronto, which was not at all a country and western town. Even the local press in Toronto was surprised by this. What was the CRTC thinking? The commissioners explained their decision with the bizarre assertion that "given the complete absence from the Toronto FM spectrum of both a country station and country music, a country musical format will contribute the most to programming diversity, to the development of Canadian talent, and to the Canadian broadcasting system as a whole."

This was, of course, nonsense. They were claiming that country and western, the whitest music ever invented, the soundtrack to every redneck life, was somehow contributing to the "diversity" of Toronto. Even Bev Oda, one of the commissioners to express a minority opinion, pointed out that "[h]istorically, Toronto audiences have not strongly supported country format radio stations. Audience surveys undertaken for applicants in these proceedings, including applicants for a country music station, indicate that dance music is preferred over country music by the overall Toronto population."

Others also pointed out the obvious: there were currently no country and western music stations in Toronto because every time someone started one, it went out of business and the owner had to change the format. This was exactly what happened to Rawlco. Very soon after start-up, the new owners turned 92.5 into yet another Top 20 station and sold it at a profit four years later.

The whole process left a sour taste in the mouths of our supporters. At that time, while all eighteen CRTC commissioners voted on applications, none of the five commissioners who actually attended the Toronto hearings voted for the winner. This smacked of behind-the-scene politics and this, along with more than one million dollars in out-of-pocket expenses for the failed bid, left most of the original group profoundly discouraged. The disappointment was compounded when the chairman of the commission, Keith Spicer, took the unprecedented step of writing a dissenting opinion stating that not only should Milestone have been awarded the licence, but that Toronto should have had a station such as ours ten years earlier.

"The decision," Spicer wrote, "ignores the music of probably 200,000 Black Torontonians, largely from the Caribbean, constituting Canada's Black community. In my view, this decision is a mistake even at the objective level of reflecting the market. The decision might have been realistic for Toronto fifteen or twenty years ago, but not now. More sadly, the decision ignores the new racial mix in Toronto, and indeed the sometimes difficult interracial climate we have seen there in recent years and months. Canada's broadcasting system must seek out opportunities to show respect and acceptance for communities which may feel insecure and left out in society."

No question, we did feel left out. Sidelined once again by the smiling and very Canadian racism of the commission majority.

Howard McCurdy, as usual, didn't mince words. He denounced the decision as "criminal to the multicultural ideal of Canada."

The dismay at the decision was felt across Toronto. A *Toronto Sun* editorial described the decision as "politically unacceptable. . . . How can the CRTC possibly maintain its integrity when its chairman and two of its most respected commissioners at the Toronto hearings disagree with the ultimate decision?"

Toronto mayor Art Eggleton picked up our cause by writing to Marcel Masse, the minister of communications, describing the decision as "regrettable not only because of the unfortunate message to members of a vital community in our City, but the people of our City as a whole will miss out on the opportunity to be exposed to an important dimension of Toronto's cultural reality. Broadcast media are an important means of fostering understanding and appreciation of our city's cosmopolitan and diverse identity. Ultimately, they should mirror the reality of Toronto."

The strength of our support among artists was shown when some of the most talented hip hop and dance music musicians joined the lobbying effort to the point of putting together an agitprop group they called Dance Appeal, which included artists such as Maestro Fresh-Wes, Michie Mee, B-Kool, Lillian Allen, Leroy Sibbles, Lorraine Scott, and Lorraine Segato from the Parachute Club. Dance Appeal recorded and performed a protest song called "CRTC (Can't Repress The Cause)," which demanded the government reverse the Rawlco decision. The song's video received blanket play on MuchMusic, and in 1991 it even won the MuchMusic Video Award for Best Dance Music Video of the Year.

With the growing outcry in our favour, we decided to launch an official challenge. Milestone requested a Cabinet review, something the Broadcasting Act allows for. We had four grounds for the appeal:

1. The strength of the dissenting CRTC opinions
2. The decision's contradiction of the CRTC's stated policy and goals
3. The regressive nature of the decision
4. The message the decision sent to the affected communities

Our appeal and the massive outpouring of support did not move the government. On October 9, 1990, the Cabinet upheld the CRTC decision and only suggested that next time it should pay attention to "the obvious desire of Torontonians for greater diversity in their broadcasters."

For most of our original investors and supporters, this final rejection by the Cabinet was one of those sobering moments that come with the realization that of course *they* would never give *us* a licence . . . a "what were we thinking?" kind of moment.

My own feeling — apart from the anger that the

government would not even respond positively to the head of CRTC, who had spoken so forcefully in our favour — was that we had to persevere. I felt a bit like I had when Conny and I were being denied service at the Miami airport restaurant on our way to Canada back in the mid-1950s. You either slink away, or you stand up and insist on your rights. I said to the others, "Let's go again. Let's make a bid so strong they will not be able to say no a second time."

But after that first failure, far fewer were willing to listen.

One thing I had learned in my life, from the soccer pitch and cricket grounds and throughout my business career, was that perseverance is one of the most important, perhaps even the most important, parts of success. Lack of perseverance does not guarantee failure, but it is the commonest cause. So I would, indeed, persevere. Although, to be honest, I did not think that it would take another decade and such a prodigious amount of time, energy, and, yes, capital, to get what we should have had in 1990.

All of this occurred while I was still mourning the deaths of my mother and Violet. Their example and their indomitable spirits made me more determined than ever to get for my community what it deserved — a voice of its own. Violet had fought for this within the Garvey-led or Garvey-inspired organizations in Toronto from the 1920s. My mother, Miss Ina, had made giving to the community a way of life. The example they had given me would not let me turn my back and walk away. If the CRTC was going to turn into the Cowboy Radio and Television Commission with their Rawlco decision, I would saddle up to take them on again.

But my father's example also made me realize that for the station to last, it would also have to be set up and run as a self-sustaining business. I was ready to risk a good deal more of my own money to pursue the licence, but the station would only survive if it was run as a business. Otherwise, it would be a very short-term venture that would last until it simply exhausted the capital of all of its investors and then faded away.

This struggle was going to take the community commitment of my mother and Violet tempered by the hard-headedness of my father. I felt I was ready to continue the battle on these terms. I just didn't know how long that battle was going to last and how difficult Canada would make it for us to find a place on the airwaves of the city.

CHAPTER THIRTEEN
WE BELIEVED AND WE DESERVED

One of the greatest aids to perseverance is not knowing how long the struggle ahead will actually be. You keep fighting, believing, or at least hoping that victory is right around the corner. In this case, right around the corner turned out to be a full decade away.

The second target radio station came into view in the early 1990s. The CKO network of all-news stations in Toronto, Ottawa, Montreal, and Quebec City foundered and closed in 1989. As well as eventually opening up a new opportunity for us, the collapse of CKO served as a cautionary tale. The network was launched in 1976 by many of the key people involved in Citytv, like Israel Switzer and David Ruskin. Despite the presence of these experienced and well-connected broadcasters, CKO managed to lose an estimated $55 million in its dozen years of existence. In Canada, even highly media savvy people like Switzer and Ruskin could lose their shirts in radio if they didn't take care of the bottom line, so those of us new to the industry had to take note of the dangers.

The CKO stations remained closed for a couple of years before the CRTC asked for recommendations on what to do with their broadcast bands: keep them as a unit or break them up and call for applications? When the Commission decided to split up the CKO network and make 99.1 available for a new Toronto station, I was ready to take the leap. But it would be with a far smaller team. Of the twenty-five Milestone Communications investors in the first round, only four others stayed on board for a second round. The five partners in this bid were me, Carl Redhead, Tony Davy, Reynold Austin, and Isaac (and later Zanana) Akande.

Carl Redhead was in many ways the heart and soul of Milestone. As a young man, he had been a teacher in his native Trinidad, and he had won a local radio announcers contest that resulted in an on-air job. He fell in love with the medium. That led him to a career as an on-air personality and, finally, as one of the very few Black radio executives in Toronto. I met him in the early 1980s, when I was launching the Black Business and Professional Association and he was vice-president and assistant general manager for Radio 1540 Limited, operator of CHIN and CHIN-FM Toronto. Carl was invited on to the BPAA executive, and at Milestone he was the resident expert of all things behind the mike. He also had a great knowledge of the workings of the CRTC and the administrative side of radio. He was one of a very few Black Canadians listed at that time in the *Who's Who*.

Tony Davy was also part of the team since day one. A communications engineer with Nortel Networks, he was our technical guy as well as our number cruncher and treasurer.

Reynold Austin was a Barbadian-born financier with his own company, Austin Global Insurance and Financial Services, who was active in the Canadian branch of the Barbadian Labour Party and in a number of community groups.

Isaac Akande, a Nigerian-born optometrist who was active in the BBPA and numerous other Black organizations, was an original partner, but he passed away shortly after our first bid. His wife, Zanana, who I mentioned earlier as one of the most powerful Black women in Toronto, agreed to continue to support the station after Isaac's death. Zanana stayed with us during her brief political career and after she resigned from the Ontario legislature in 1994. She continued to make an important contribution to Milestone for another decade and also played an important role in the Black community as an advocate for social justice.

Another key member of the team was Bob Buchan, the Rogers broadcasting lawyer. An excellent counsellor, he knew all of the commissioners and most of the major broadcasters, and also understood and shared our goals for a Black radio station with his own commitment to racial and social justice. We also had a young media-industry lawyer who would stay with us to the end, Carolyn Stamegna. She helped us put together our bid in a way that ensured that we jumped through all of the CRTC hoops.

From the outset, I knew that one of the essential ingredients we would need if we were to have a hope of winning a voice for ourselves was that the whole community pull together. When I was given a Harry Jerome award in 1996, I touched on this in my acceptance speech:

> Brothers and sisters, as we approach the end of the twentieth century, we are in a struggle for survival, for opportunities, for recognition. And though we have been here since 1603, and fighting and dying for this country since 1812, when a Black regiment turned back the American forces at Queenston Bridge, we are still largely excluded from the media and even national discussions concerning the future of our country.
>
> We need greater unity among the Black diaspora, among Trinidadians, Continental Africans, Antiguans, Black Canadians, Jamaicans . . . all of our people. Nothing to which we aspire individually will allow us to move forward as a people, as proud Black People, until we unite.

As it turned out, that call for unity would be answered in the community over our second bid for a radio licence. And we would need all the community help we could get because, we soon learned, CBC Radio was making a bid for the same FM station we were, claiming that their 740 AM signal couldn't be heard in parts of the city. In the first bid against Rawlco, it seemed at worst a David and David battle between us. This time, with CBC in the running, it was definitely Milestone's David against CBC's Goliath.

In some sectors of Canadian society, the voice of the CBC is the voice of God, and we worried from the outset that the fix might be in. In all of the main markets — Toronto, Ottawa, Montreal, and Quebec City — CBC was making bids for the CKO stations. Still, we went ahead with the process, taking the CRTC on its word that it would be fair and open. To turn the odds in our favour, we would need to create a war room that would enlist not only our individual connections but our entire community to fight what was essentially a political battle.

Recognizing that the term "Black music" seemed to frighten the CRTC during our first bid, we decided to use instead the euphemism of the all-encompassing "world urban contemporary" music, which in the music industry at the time was actually synonymous with Black music. To help clarify this for the CTRC members, we spelled out what world urban contemporary or Black music was:

> . . . a universally recognized identification for a style of popular music which created a rhythmic musical underpinning to what was once standard, smooth, popular music . . . the style is heralded and sung by numerous white performers as well, so much so that Black Music has been recognized as being the music style that has influenced the birth of rock music . . . Ancestrally, Black Music has its roots in African rhythms. As every musicologist knows, wherever slavery of old transported Africans to a new land, there eventually developed such rhythms as the Jazz of America, the Samba of Brazil, the Calypso of

the Caribbean, the Blues and the Rhythm and Blues of Black America, numerous Latin rhythms such as Bossa Nova and the Merengue: although these last mentioned, were hybridized with European elements such as Spanish and Portuguese influences.

We opened a new Milestone office on Bay Street and worked night and day to raise both money and support in the community. I spent all my free time speaking to Black community groups in Toronto, urging them to send letters to the CRTC demanding a Black station for the city. The community responded in a way they never had before to any issue other than the police shootings. They sent in thousands of letters to support the station, and virtually every night there was an invitation for me to speak to another group. Young and old, the community backed our bid and I was proud to be part of it.

Then, six weeks into the process, the fix we feared was confirmed: CBC announced its interest in the station and Heritage Minister Sheila Copps, whose department controlled the CRTC, ordered a stop to the process and announced all of the licences would be awarded to the CBC stations. After a moment of stunned silence, there was a chorus of denunciation from all of the bidders, who collectively had spent hundreds of thousands of dollars, perhaps even millions, in a process that was suddenly, arbitrarily, terminated by the minister. The terminated bidders, who included heavyweights like Rogers, descended on local Liberal MPs and cabinet ministers to complain, and they were backed by local press. We then threatened Copps with a collective lawsuit to get back the money we had wasted on the aborted process.

Realizing the political mess she had created with the pre-emptive strike in favour of CBC, the Minister suddenly backtracked and reinstated the CRTC process. But by that time, it was a poisoned atmosphere. The CRTC was responsible to the heritage minister, and she had let everyone know that she was determined to give these stations to the CBC. All we could do was play out our hand. And finally we decided to do so. To the bitter end. We would not make it easy for the government to toss us aside after we spent so much time, effort, and money on their on-again, off-again bid process, and we would do our best to ensure that the Liberals would pay a political price.

Of the twelve competitors, Milestone was recognized as a front-runner along with CBC; it is a tribute to our bid that even with Copps in their corner, CBC felt the need to go all out to try to defeat us. CBC did a mailing from Thornhill to the lakeshore and used all of their eight media outlets, TV and radio stations, in all of the bid cities to beat the bushes for support from their audiences. In the end, they received 4,500 letters of support.

Our bid, funded out of our own pockets and with an enormous amount of sweat equity, garnered more than three times as many letters of support than the CBC. In fact, our 14,000 letters were and remain a record for any bid before the CRTC. To our delight, and I must admit our surprise given the negative press our community generally received in the mainstream media, the Milestone bid was again supported by editorials of Toronto's three major newspapers.

Down to the wire, we lacked only the initial cash for operations and that was provided at the last minute by a $300,000 note from a venture capital company where a friend of ours, Joe de Tuba, worked. It was one of those nail-biting moments on the night before the deadline when we still didn't have a bank guarantee. We knew we would get it soon but we didn't yet have it, so Joe took his bank's letterhead and wrote us the letter of guarantee and we made the deadline. During the next phase, when the CRTC sent back a list of deficiencies in the bids, they asked, essentially, who the hell Joe de Tuba was, but by that time our operating capital loan was covered, and we could send back the updated information.

We finished the bid in the early hours of the morning and decided that I would personally take the eleven copies to Ottawa to make sure they were there on time. In the morning, I had the copies printed and bundled together, and I flew to Ottawa in the early afternoon. At the check-in, they looked at the bulky bag of copies that I was carrying along with my briefcase and said I would have to check it in as baggage. I shrugged. What were the chances that they would lose it? I checked it in and less than two hours later I watched the slowly emptying luggage carousel at the Ottawa airport spin around and around without our briefs. When it was clear that they were not on that plane, I took a cab to the CRTC, whose office was closing in a couple of hours, to tell them what had happened. They were, I must admit, gracious about it. They said that if it came on a later flight, I could bring it to security and get a receipt for it and it would be considered to have arrived on time. I returned to the airport to spend the rest of the day watching the spinning carousel until my package finally arrived. I grabbed it before it had finished sliding from the conveyor belt to the edge of the carousel and rushed it to CRTC security. It was done.

We had crossed the finish line. We were all proud of our accomplishment and convinced, more than ever, that our bid, supported by virtually the entire Black community and with most of the Toronto media establishment behind it, deserved to win. We were just as certain that we would not, because the winner had been decided before the race even started.

No one was at all surprised when the CRTC gave the Toronto frequency and all of the open frequencies to CBC. The only real surprise was how close we had come: the commissioners had split 3–2.

Commissioner Callahan noted in his support for Milestone's application that

> The CBC has not made a compelling case, within the appropriateness and efficiency requirements of the *Broadcasting Act*, for awarding the frequency 99.1 MHz to the Corporation to improve reception for some of its listeners in the Toronto area.
>
> An appropriate and efficient use of the frequency 99.1 MHz in the sense of the Broadcasting Act is proposed in the application of B. Denham Jolly, OBCI (the Milestone group). It would provide the opportunity for members of a large and diverse segment of the Toronto multicultural community to reflect their cultures on their own terms and in their own way, and

a particular voice for Toronto's black music, artistic and business communities.

Commissioner Gail Scott said she agreed with Callahan "that the application from the Milestone Group would best serve the public interest in Canada's largest city."

The final decision against us, even if it was close, released a wave of anger that we'd kept in check as we went through the motions of fighting for our bid. It came from our team, from the thousands and thousands of Toronto Blacks who saw their hopes dashed for having our own voice, and from the larger community of Toronto who saw, plainly, the abuse of power coming from the backroom manipulations of a process. It was as though Copps had said, "If you want a hearing we will give you a hearing, but no way you are getting that radio station."

The Liberal Party arrogance during this period was truly astonishing. At one point, I went with a group from Milestone to lobby David Collenette, then the Liberal minister responsible for Toronto, and he sat there with his feet on his desk, listening while we made our case to the soles of his shoes.

In a lobbying effort with one of the ministers, the famous Liberal rainmaker Keith Davey was sitting in, and when I said that Liberals should listen to the Black community because 75% of us voted for the party, Davey smugly interjected: "More like 90%!"

But even after the announcement, we didn't give up. The government decision was being questioned, often bitterly so. *Toronto Star* columnists from Royson James to Dalton

Camp condemned it. Royson said that the message from the CRTC to the Black community was, "Just go away, plan your little dances and street parties and once-a-year Caribana, if you can manage that, and don't bother us . . ." It makes you want to howl.

Dalton Camp, himself a national CBC commentator, wrote that "[n]o one, surely, could be unsympathetic to the Milestone application, or ignorant of its powerful value to the whole community."

We were determined to ride the continuing wave of support. I kept on visiting community groups to talk about the Liberal Party treason to our community and tried in a very public way to drive a wedge between Black voters and the Liberals because I knew this, more than anything, would get the Liberals' attention.

At the same time, Liberal members sympathetic to us spoke quietly to the minister to underline the injustice of denying the Black community a voice when we had put together a remarkably good bid and the damage this injustice was doing to community relations in Toronto. These criticisms had some resonance with Copps' team because they knew they had mishandled the file to the point of putting the whole process into disrepute. Their initial solution, however, was to try to throw us off by playing a bait-and-switch game.

We were quietly told by David Collenette that the Cabinet, to correct the situation, would offer Milestone a 93.5 FM "drop in" frequency. Ironically, this was the frequency we had suggested the CBC use during the hearings. The announcement of 93.5 for Milestone would be made soon, we were told, but first Milestone had to write a letter saying we were pleased with the decision and the process Copps had followed. We made our official application for the new frequency and dutifully wrote the letter praising the government.

Then, on the day of the press conference, our appeal was suddenly and inexplicably disallowed. But the government went ahead and used our letter to say we were happy with the process. I was devastated. In fact, I was flabbergasted. I had heard a lot about politicians, but this trickery surpassed my wildest imaginings.

It also gave me more ammunition with which to attack the government. I continued to speak out against the government at every opportunity. When I was given an award by the Black Action Defence Committee, I even turned that into an occasion to beat on the Liberals, although I was careful to exempt my long-time friend and ally Jean Augustine.

"I thought I would have been able to report tonight that Milestone has a licensed FM radio station," I told the gathering of Black activists. "But unfortunately, not only was that decision stolen from us by a blatant abuse of process . . . this bogus hearing . . . the federal Liberals, led by Sheila Copps and David Collenette, in spite of great effort by Jean Augustine, recognized that it meant empowerment, a fulfillment of the dreams, hopes, and aspirations of an entire community. It meant self-determination for Blacks. So they changed their minds. In October 1997, they told Milestone to drop dead."

In my speeches I would also go after Jean Chrétien and the Liberal vote by comparing his government unfavourably to the previous Progressive Conservative one.

"Jean Chrétien continues, in my view, to make Brian Mulroney look good," I would say. "Mulroney appointed Lincoln Alexander as Lieutenant Governor of Ontario, Senator Oliver to the Senate, Glenda Sims to head of status of women, Gail Scott head of Federal Civil Service, Julius Isaac chief justice of the federal court, Emmy Mascol to a five-year term on board of the CNR . . . So next time you see the Right Honorable Jean Chrétien, you may want to ask what has he done for us lately? Although you may have trouble finding him; he's only glimpsed the Black community once in the past eight years . . . People are always falling over themselves to vote Liberal, and for what?"

We sent out a flyer into the community exclaiming that the struggle continued and calling on them to continue the battle with us. Under the heading "What you can do to help" they were asked to:

1. Call the Prime Minister's office
2. Write the Prime Minister
3. Call or write your local MP
4. Call the newspapers
5. Write a letter to the editor to the newspapers
6. Make copies of this flyer and hand it out to family and friends
7. Call Milestone to volunteer

To make it easier, we provided them with all the addresses and numbers to write and call, and we asked that they fax a copy of all of their correspondence on the issue to Milestone and to David Collenette's office in Toronto. We were overwhelmed by the response. We later heard that Collenette was, too, and he had to get a new fax line for his office because our supporters were keeping his fax occupied day and night with letters of protest. His wife, Penny, was Chrétien's director of appointments, so the waves we were making in Collenette's office in Toronto were definitely being felt in the PMO.

Our fight against the government even began to draw international attention. I was contacted by the *Washington Post* about our struggle with the CRTC, and they used this story as the centrepiece of an article exploring what they found was the widespread hypocrisy of Canadians and the Canadian government over race.

In snappy journalistic style, the article began:

> Surfing the local radio dial, Jamaican native Denham Jolly identified what to him seemed two obvious shortcomings in this most diverse of Canada's cities — the lack of a local rap, jazz, and world-beat station that reflected the city's multiracial population and the lack of any black owners in the local broadcasting industry. He thought he could tackle both issues by developing his own proposal for Toronto's sole remaining FM licence, and he entered a recent competition for it with high hopes and a large dose of community backing.

What he discovered, he says now, is that Canada's cherished official ideal of diversity sometimes has its limits. . . .

In a nation that prides itself on diversity and visualizes its society as a "mosaic" of equal pieces, the distribution of political, social, and economic influence is still largely held by those of European heritage.

"Canadians say they believe in the mosaic, but some of the tiles have never seen a polish from the day they were put on the wall," said Jolly. "There is a lot of lip service, but in matters of race you are never quite sure of your place."

The paper then delved a little deeper into the hypocrisy in the Canadian soul. "It can be seen in the country's largely white governing institutions — the handful of non-white faces, for example, among the 56 recently elected city council members in Toronto, a city some estimate to be more than 40 percent non-white — or in the lack of racial diversity in the nation's corporate head offices. In the *Financial Post* magazine's recent survey of Canada's top 200 corporate chief executives, only seven are non-white. Of those, five are Japanese or Chinese natives running subsidiaries of Japanese- or Chinese-owned companies; the other two are Asians who built their own businesses in Canada."

The article then listed the poverty, wage, and job statistics that reflected the very real dollars-and-cents racism in Canada. And this discrimination "can be seen in the head tables when Canada's elite convene. When Britain's Queen Elizabeth II visited last summer, she spoke approvingly of the Canadian mosaic — a word Canadians use to distinguish their country from an American 'melting pot' they think demands too much conformity. But when the queen took her place among 16 head-table guests at a state dinner in her honour, the only non-white representatives of that mosaic were jazz pianist Oscar Peterson and his wife."

I was pleased to see the *Washington Post* linking our difficulty getting a radio licence to the broader issue of race in Canada. Because while we were publicly slamming the government, we were also appealing to Cabinet directly to reverse the decision, and the *Post* article provided additional leverage. We were also greatly aided by having Jean Augustine on the inside. As mentioned, I was used to working with Jean on Toronto causes: When her elections came up, I helped out as a donor and even made sure her volunteers had pizzas to fuel themselves into the night. On election day, I drove people to the polls. Now that I was railing against the Liberal Party from without, she was quietly working from the inside, arranging meetings between Sheila Copps and our Ottawa lawyers in her office and speaking out in favour of us around the Cabinet table. Finally, our rebellion paid off. In 1999, after two years of determined shaking and almost a dozen years since we began our quest, the fruit fell from the tree.

It was only a year before the federal election when the federal Cabinet issued an order in council to the CRTC directing it to give precedence to applications that took into account Toronto's cultural and racial diversity. There was a quick call for new applications for the "drop in" frequency of 93.5 FM. The same five Milestone partners decided to apply once more with the same legal, engineering, and research team.

One major change in this application is that, on the advice of Bob Buchan, we brought in an established broadcaster as a minority partner. The company was the leader in the industry, Standard Broadcasting, then owned by Allan and Gary Slaight, who had purchased the company from Conrad Black in 1985. They would have a 29% ownership but with only one voting share.

We were helped in securing the Standard partnership by Finlay MacDonald, who we hired to give us some additional backroom heft. Finlay was an Ottawa mover and shaker who was the consummate political and media insider. He had joined CJCH radio in Edmonton after the war and later became station president. He was, for a time, president of the Canadian Association of Broadcasters. In 1961, he was one of the founding directors of the CTV Television Network. He retained his family ties to the Progressive Conservative Party by running for the party in 1963; after losing the election, he served as president of the Nova Scotia Progressive Conservative Party. He was the chief of staff for both Robert Stanfield and Joe Clark and chairman of the Brian Mulroney transition committee. Mulroney appointed him to the Senate in 1984, and he resigned in 1998 to work as a lobbyist.

I remember introducing him during a meeting as "our spin doctor . . . the man other spin doctors ask for advice to get extra spin." And true to form, Finlay worked his magic for us in the halls of power, and he helped secure Standard Broadcasting as a minority partner. Sadly, Finlay and I had a falling out when he demanded Milestone give him a consultancy contract in the hundreds-of-thousands-of-dollars range, which was way more than we could afford. When I told him this, he reacted angrily, blurting out, "I made you guys."

It was an unfortunate thing to say, and I was stung by it. We had had good relations to that point — Finlay had even visited me in Jamaica. But after that remark, both our business relationship and friendship cooled. Still, I was very sorry to hear of his death in 2002 because I had hoped we could, in time, repair our friendship.

There was also one additional wrinkle: a competing bid for an almost identical format station from Arnold Auguste, the publisher of *Share*. His bid was backed by only 250 letters of support — against our 1,200 this time — and most of the capital for his bid came from a Newfoundland company that had made money in used cars and newspapers and was looking for a way into the Toronto media market. An article in the *National Post Business* magazine tried to invent a long-time feud between Arnold and me, since I had been publisher of his competition at *Contrast*, but nothing could be further from the truth. Our bid was our only preoccupation; we were not looking sideways at the competition but were keeping our attention on our own bid and our eyes on the goal.

The hearing was held at the Triumph Hotel at Keele and the 401 in February 2000, and our presentation, I must say, was flawless. We proposed "a diverse, cosmopolitan music format based on rhythm and blues (R&B) music and related genres . . . the modern-day reflection of the rich musical traditions of Black musicians and Black-influenced music over at least the past century."

"This application," we said, "reflects the continuing efforts of the five founding members of Milestone over the past decade to achieve their shared vision of a new radio station that fills an important musical niche in the Toronto radio market, that provides a showcase for the unique and innovative music that is being created and performed by Canadian musical artists in clubs and concert halls throughout the city, and which gives members of the Black community their own voice in the Canadian broadcasting system."

We even had blues legend Salome Bey appear before the committee to tell the commissioners that "it is very important that you support Milestone. It is more than important. I hate the thought of you sitting there thinking that I am begging, but I do see you kind of waking up and getting a little rhythm. You will get a lot of that from Milestone . . . Let's not have to come here again. Let this be it."

This time the commissioners seemed to get it. But they had seemed to get it before, only for us to find our bid overruled in backrooms in Ottawa, so we once again hoped for the best and expected the worst. The deliberation dragged on. On the second week of June, we were still waiting, and I decided on a Thursday evening to head to New York for an extended weekend.

I was staying at the Roosevelt Hotel on 45th and Madison. It was Friday morning, and I was having my coffee and looking down at the people far below streaming out of

Grand Central Station on foot while the traffic was in its permanent state of gridlock reaching all the way to the United Nations Plaza five blocks away. I was contemplating the bizarrely functional chaos of Manhattan when the phone rang.

On the other end, the sweetest French accented voice I ever heard said, "Monsieur Jolly, I'm doing what I wanted to do ten years ago. You have been awarded the frequency of 93.5 FM to broadcast in Toronto. Congratulations and good luck."

That was it.

A twelve-year struggle — one that had taken more money than I would like to admit to spending and an incredible measure of sweat and tears — was over.

We had broken through. We had won. Not me. Our community. We had won the right to have a voice in the mix of Canadian voices, something that we had always, in so many ways, been refused before. But we had persevered; we had fought, and we had won.

I was proud of our team, but I also thought of Violet Blackman and Harry Gairey. They had been struggling since the 1920s to build a small space on College Street where Blacks, especially Black youth, could meet and speak to each other in the midst of that too-often-unfriendly city. Now we were growing that space into the airwaves that reached across all of Metropolitan Toronto and allowed us to speak not only among ourselves but to the larger community. At last young people would know that they were not isolated in someone else's city. Toronto was theirs and they would have a clear, loud voice in it.

This was not a time to be in New York.

I picked up the phone and changed my reservation to the first flight heading back to Toronto. Then I called the Milestone office. While I was in the air, the Milestone secretary was calling around to organize a victory party for friends and supporters.

It was when I arrived back in Toronto that I came to understand how deep our support was in the city.

The *Toronto Star* and the *Globe and Mail* had supported Milestone's struggle from the beginning and covered the final CRTC decision in detail. A *Toronto Star* editorial said "Finally . . . the CRTC granted the city's strong Black community a spot on the FM dial. Friday's decision was a well-earned victory for Denham Jolly, president of Milestone Communications, who was twice rebuffed by the CRTC."

The *Toronto Sun*, a newspaper that did not have a reputation of being friendly, or even fair, to the Black community, was even more effusive. "At long last, the dinosaurs at the Canadian Radio-television and Telecommunications Commission have admitted Toronto needs a Black-owned, urban format station on the FM dial."

The *Sun* even managed to see itself reflected in our victory. "After all, 29 years ago the *Sun* was the upstart in town, offering a fresh new voice to anyone who would listen and fighting for a niche alongside old, established rivals. So welcome to the fray, Milestone. It's about time. This decision is music to our ears."

It was music to everyone's ears. Even Arnold Auguste, a competitor to our bid, warmly congratulated us in the pages of *Share*.

That night, I was surrounded by our jubilant team, friends, and supporters. Wine and beer flowed; an incredible spread of food was set out. Music played loud, and this being an urban radio crowd, the air had the sweet smell of marijuana. This was a celebration of a hard-fought victory.

I remember introducing the team by saying, "Milestone shares your joy. Milestone shares your triumph. It took twelve years but we did it! As Shirley MacLaine has said, you can accomplish anything if you believe in it and you deserve it. Ladies and gentlemen, we believed and we deserved!"

CHAPTER FOURTEEN

NUMBER ONE CONTEMPORARY RADIO
STATION IN CANADA

Then the morning after.

The CRTC had given us a year to get on air, and there seemed to be ten years' worth of work ahead. We had to get right to work on giving content and form to the dream. More than once during this period, the expression "be careful what you wish for" crossed my mind.

On one hand, there were the nuts and bolts. We had to scout around for office and studio space, and we found a well-located office on the fifth floor of the new 111 Yonge Street Tower, just across from the Eaton Centre. Then we had to hire specialists to design and build the recording studios and begin the search for affordable recording equipment. Launching a radio station, I quickly learned, would involve a constant juggling of the financial, engineering, and artistic.

From the very beginning, we were flooded with applications to work for us. FLOW 93.5 was the talk of the town in media circles, and I was gratified to see young people from all ethnic backgrounds knocking at our door. One application that naturally caught my eye was from my daughter, Nicole. She had the credentials. She had graduated from the London School of Economics in 1993 with a master's in social behaviour and had been hired by Goldfarb Consultants, where she had worked her way up to marketing vice-president responsible for the international Ford Motor Company account, among others. We hired her to set up the marketing plan for the station and went to work building our on-air team.

In those initial months, our close-knit group included Carl, Nicole, and Marion Snow, my secretary at Tyndall for twenty years, who suddenly found herself in the radio business. Fil Fraser, Harry Jerome's biographer, was also part of the team.

Fil was born into Montreal's tiny Black community in 1932 and had become a pioneer in radio for Black Canadians. He was first hired by Foster Hewitt at CKFH in Toronto when he was only nineteen years old, and he went on to a number of radio jobs and a career in Western Canada as a journalist and author — besides the Jerome biography, he has also written *How the Blacks Created Canada*. He worked as a film producer and served as president of Vision TV. At one time, he even served as the Human Rights Commissioner in Alberta.

In those station start-up days, I was working very closely with Fil, Carl, and Nicole as we began putting

The original management team at FLOW 93.5: Aisha Wickham, Michelle Price, me, Farley Flex, and my daughter, Nicole.

together both the management and the on-air team. We worked, it sometimes seemed, around the clock, getting together early in the day for a breakfast meeting and remaining together for dinner while we worked into the night assembling the thousands of small technical and material cogs of a broadcasting machine and hiring the human resources to run it.

The senior management team we gradually assembled included Michelle Price, Farley Flex, Aisha Wickham, and

Keith Davis, with Sylvia Searles serving as senior policy advisor.

Michelle Price, a Georgia native, was hired as program director. She had experience in urban radio in Memphis, Tennessee, and Fort Wayne, Texas, definite ideas of where to take the station, and a straight ahead no-nonsense approach that helped us quickly get out of the gate. Farley Flex, manager to the hip hop star Maestro, was a top music promoter in Toronto; we hired him as music director. Aisha Wickham, who was firmly rooted in the Black community and was working for the City of Toronto in an economic development project, became our spoken word and new media director. Keith Davis, a former Standard Broadcasting ad salesman, became our general sales manager.

Sylvia Searles was a volunteer but still an important part of the team. Her Barbadian-born father had been one of the first Black lawyers in Toronto, and she had worked as a senior advisor in the office of three-term Toronto mayor David Miller, so she brought a great deal of political sophistication to the station.

And, of course, the Slaight family, Allan and Gary, owners of our minority partner Standard Broadcasting, were there in the backroom — and occasionally trying to push their way into the front room. Especially Gary, who was used to running the show and who I found occasionally seemed to think he was in charge at FLOW. I remember in a moment of exasperation I said to him, to try to get him to back off, "You are not my father!"

I'm not sure why I used that particular epithet; but after he got over his surprise, he understood what I was trying to say and he backed off. We became friends as well as partners.

The Slaights were a remarkable story in themselves. Allan was a broadcast legend who, as program director, transformed Toronto's CHUM into a pop-music radio success in the 1950s and '60s. Then he and his son, Gary, moved into station ownership in the 1970s and '80s, helming the largest network in the country after their 1985 purchase of Standard Broadcasting, which by then was being run by Gary as CEO. While he did, on occasion, still step on my toes, Gary also was there for advice when I needed it, and I will always appreciate him and Allan for their indispensable help in setting up the station.

In the end, it took our hard-working team less than the CRTC-mandated year to get on the air. By February 2001, we were ready to go live, with all of our work converging toward that moment. The studio floor and walls and ceiling had been soundproofed, and the equipment that we acquired with help from CHUM Ltd. had been installed. Working with Michelle Price, our program was developed to contain a uniquely Canadian mix of R&B, hip hop, soul, reggae, calypso, soca, world & Latin "old school," highlife, jazz, and gospel. The top-level staff, I was happy to say, consisted mostly of women, and our entire team reflected our target audience and the city overall, consisting of people from twelve different nations. And the whole endeavour was still firmly under the control of the members of the Black community who had launched it. Nicole had developed a marketing strategy around our groundbreaking presence on the scene, and Keith was out booking ads for day one. For on-air talent, we were lucky enough to get the Winnipeg-born comedy legend Kenny Robinson for our flagship FLOW 93.5 *Morning Rush* program.

And, of course, we held a "flick the switch" party. It was at the Capitol Centre at Yonge and Eglinton on the evening of February 9, 2001, the first day we went live on 93.5 MHz with effective radiated power of 298 watts. The first song we played was Bob Marley's iconoclastic hit "Roots, Rock, Reggae," and we were, indeed, "bubblin'." At the party that evening, I spoke about the staff who had come out of the gate with impressive amounts of energy, expertise, and creativity to get us on air ahead of schedule.

But I also reminded the team of our larger mission. "Milestone will help create important artists and for that we have set aside $2.1 million to be used over the seven years of our licence. Milestone will conduct talent searches, produce live concerts, help fund Caribana, provide journalism scholarships for minority youth, and stage free events . . . Two great imperatives, social and economic, thereby creating a greater effective demand in our community."

I also mentioned that we would be working closely with the existing media outlets for the Black community — *Share, Pride, Caribbean Camera, The Gleaner, Word Magazine*. And I reminded everyone that, in fulfilling our mission, we still had to be mindful that Milestone was a business and had to operate it as such. Otherwise we would lose it — and all of the good it could do for our community.

So the whirlwind of FLOW 93.5 was let loose on the world. Nicole and her marketing department had saturated the Toronto market with a series of stylish print and TV ads that let the city know that, yes, this was a Black-run station,

An early print ad for FLOW 93.5.

announcing our arrival. And way ahead of schedule, we climbed into the middle of the pack in Toronto. Within weeks of our launch, we found ourselves in the position of fielding calls from agents and publicists for Black artists passing through Toronto looking for on-air interviews. Our studios at 111 Yonge Street would end up hosting the biggest names in pop culture: Alicia Keys, Jay Z, Beyoncé, Kanye West, Lady Gaga, and many others. In fact, everyone who was anyone in Urban music would pass through the doors for an interview to promote their work. From the beginning, FLOW was seen as a trendsetter in the Toronto market, and it began to attract not only musicians but Black football and basketball stars like Chris Bosh who also saw their culture reflected in the station. Finally, there was a Black voice that reached the length and breadth of Toronto. *Contrast* had reached thousands in our community; FLOW 93.5 would reach hundreds of thousands, including many in the larger community who would finally get to know us not through their outmoded stereotypes but through our own voices.

Within a year, our reach was greatly expanded when we filed an application with the CRTC for a technical amendment to increase our Effective Radiated Power (ERP) from 298 to 1,430 watts, which the CRTC granted. In 2002, we applied for a digital radio licence that would enabled us to provide an ERP of 5,084 watts to reach a broader audience and with a clearer sound than standard radio could offer, and this was also granted. We were then in a position to become a major presence on the Greater Toronto Area airwaves. In terms of coverage, FLOW reached from Port Hope in the east to Niagara Falls in the west, and north to Cookstown, ten miles south of Barrie, which gave us a potential market of six million people. Our community, and all of the Toronto region, would hear us loud and clear. By then we were also live streaming on the internet, and I used to tune in even when I was out of town — an amazing feeling.

Then the unexpected happened. When industry leaders saw what to them seemed like the immediate success of urban radio in Toronto, they started making bids for similar stations in Vancouver, Calgary, and Edmonton. After losing for twelve years, we were now winners, trendsetters to be not only emulated but brought on board to give other bids credibility. The first to request our involvement were the Slaights, who asked me to personally endorse the Standard Broadcasting bid for an urban station in Calgary. I said I would do it, but as a representative of Milestone and not as an individual. Eventually, I agreed to be on the board of CIBK FM 98.5 The Vibe, in exchange for Milestone receiving 5% of valuation after seven years. I helped with their pitch, and they got the Calgary licence.

A short time after that, Toronto's legendary CHUM FM approached me to be part of a fifty-fifty partnership for an application for an urban station in the Edmonton market. I accepted on behalf of Milestone, and the new station took on the name 91.7 FM The Bounce. I appeared before the CRTC to explain what we had done with FLOW in Toronto, how we had brought Toronto listeners a whole new sound and advertisers a new access to the hard-to-reach youth demographic, the most diverse in the city. At the time, our listeners were 40% Black and 60% other racial groups including, of course, a large portion of hip young whites.

Urban radio, we had proved, was a viable commercial format in Canada. By then the stations in Vancouver and Calgary had joined FLOW near the top of the pack in the key twelve-to-twenty-four demographic. We used the

Rap stars Michie Mee and Maestro showing
their support for FLOW 93.5.

Toronto model for the Edmonton station, getting 5,300 individual letters of support from the community.

Competitors for the Edmonton licence accused us of a cookie-cutter approach across Canada. I reassured the committee that, far from it, The Bounce would be as representative of Edmonton as FLOW was of Toronto. The station would build up a multi-million-dollar Canadian talent development, a specific portion of which would go to Edmonton-based artists. The CRTC finally understood that the market across Canada, including Edmonton, was ready for Black and, more generally, urban music, and The Bounce was awarded a licence.

The sailing wasn't always easy, though. And it was made more difficult in Toronto when we lost one of the station's most important steersmen, Carl Redhead, whose health had been fragile for some time as he fought what would be a losing battle against cancer.

When Carl died in December 2002, I lost more than a colleague and business partner. He was a true friend, someone I went to for advice on issues in business and in life. He was one of the first people to commit to bringing Canada's first urban radio station to fruition. For twelve long years, Carl worked tirelessly on the project. He even gave up his senior management position at CHIN in June 2000. He was a hugely respected expert in the rules and regulations of the CRTC, so much so that the commission even consulted with him on a number of issues. He took pride in the fact that FLOW 93.5 was holding its own in the competitive Toronto market. Carl was a quiet warrior, withstanding the physical rigours of his illness while he dedicated himself to the major undertaking of launching a new radio station.

Nicole, with her Goldfarb and professional business experience, would eventually replace him as vice-president, operations. And she would face some big challenges, most notably the grumblings in the community about the programming: parts of the Caribbean Black community thought the station should be running non-stop Caribbean music.

Many times I had to explain to individuals and groups that the station had to be run as a business or we would very quickly lose it. Our programmer, Michelle Price, had been told from the outset that in order to meet our revenue goals, she had to get us at least in the middle of the pack in listenership. That meant programming, along with R&B, blues, spiritual, reggae and other Afro-Caribbean music, a significant amount of hip hop and related musical styles that were dominating the airwaves around the world. It was a new and exciting Black music genre, and this was what young people, particularly young Blacks, wanted to hear. So it fit perfectly with our mission.

But many Caribbean Blacks imagined that since I was Jamaican-born and many of the backers were from the Islands, we would simply create a transplanted Caribbean station. And while we did make a point of including a very significant amount of Caribbean music on our playlist, it was not our mainstay. Our cause was not always helped by Michelle's sometimes overly direct manner; her talent as a programmer was somewhat undermined by her weakness in diplomacy. But I tried to explain to the community groups the reasons behind our programming decisions and how we always had to balance the artistic and the financial. The former made the station worthwhile, but the latter made it sustainable.

In community meetings, I was up front about it. "The economic reality is that FLOW is a stand-alone station. It does not have a sister AM, it has no stable of AMs and FMs to benefit from economy of scale. FLOW has to grind it out day by day for survival in the fiercest radio market in Canada, which is also the largest radio market in North America."

I would remind our people that "FLOW is an urban station with a licence to play urban music. We are not a reggae station, although we do have *Riddim Tracks* on Sundays, and we also play one tune per hour. Nor are we a calypso station, although we have *Soca Therapy* on Sundays. To compete with Rogers, which has thirty-nine stations, we must play smart by testing the music through focus groups before it goes on the air. Radio is measured three times a year by the Bureau of Broadcast Measurement. Without

Drake, with the Programming and Marketing departments.

that listenership share number, the advertising agencies are not interested in buying time on your station."

Our programming brought in the revenues that allowed us not only to stay on the air but to spend millions of dollars to help develop Canadian artists over the seven years of our licence, the majority of it on visible-minority kids, helping them rise from garage bands to national and international stars. We were the first Toronto station to play Drake and many others who have become international household names. CRTC rules required us to play around 30% Canadian content, but very early on we reached and surpassed that goal, something almost unheard of in commercial Toronto radio at the time.

We also broke new ground with staffing. Prior to February 2001, there were only two Blacks in radio sales in the whole country, and zero working as music directors, program directors, or station managers. During our start-up and throughout the decade, we mentored young Black technicians, sales managers, program directors, and station directors to ensure they had a place not only at our station but in the Canadian industry as a whole.

The grumbling continued, but more faintly now, as the community understood that we were not a volunteer college campus type of station but a highly professional operation in a killer market. Our management team knew that if they didn't look after the business side, all would be for naught. We would lose the station. None of its backers could afford to keep an operation with more than fifty employees alive for long if the revenues were not there — it would quickly burn through our capital and go silent. These were the realities. Fortunately, most of our original supporters understood this, and the radio station quickly moved into the black — even a little ahead of schedule.

But our commitment to the community was unquestionable, and at board meetings we often asked what more we could do with the station to help the community. Our young people, especially in places like the Jane-Finch neighbourhood, were still battling for survival against a world that was telling them in so many ways that they were not wanted. At the station, we instituted internship programs for Black students that allowed them to be exposed to a commercial radio station that celebrated their culture and to receive hands-on training and experience, and we funded minority scholarships at Ryerson. But we knew that we had to do more. The world was changing again, you could feel it in the air, and it was not changing for the better.

While we were building FLOW, there was a palpable American-style coarsening of the discourse in Canada around poverty, with an "us and them" mentality replacing compassion. Wealth was rising to the top and the middle and lower classes were sinking. This feeling was borne out by statistics, which showed that the gap between rich and poor was growing as more and more Canadians were driven into the kind of poverty that creeps up and steals hope and dignity and casts a long shadow on people's ability to provide for their children. It brings fear and dismay about tomorrow, and these feelings were increasing across the city.

The Mike Harris Conservative gang was in power in Ontario, instituting its slash-and-burn economics. The government, among other things, cut welfare to single mothers and cut water inspections leading to the mass E. coli poisoning in Walkerton. It was reckless stupidity. School programs were slashed, ESL programs were eliminated, youth counsellors were laid off, and zero-tolerance policies were imposed in the schools, so teachers had to expel kids who were difficult to discipline. It was a recipe for disaster, driving kids onto the streets without the tools to survive.

The impoverishment of Canada's children, of all races, was the most unforgivable aspect, and it was something I denounced often in my speeches to community groups during this period. I would quote statistics. In 1989, the House of Commons voted unanimously to eliminate child poverty by the year 2000. But several years later, there were actually 500,000 more poor children in Canada. Today the situation is worse, and I have always made the case that poverty is not only harmful for the victims, it is harmful for society as a whole — countries with large disparities between rich and poor will not prosper in the long term. In a wealthy country like Canada, poverty is inexcusable because it is so obviously avoidable.

We heard a lot of talk about the deficit; indeed, we were asked to starve our children to pay off the deficit. Yet after the deficit was eliminated, we were still being asked to make sacrifices to pay down the debt and, often, to cut taxes on businesses and the wealthiest individuals.

The brunt of the neo-liberal mean-spiritedness was felt by Toronto's Black community. I was involved with the Jane Finch Concerned Citizens Organization all through this period, and I was occasionally invited to speak to them. The first time was in 1998 when the group had won the Unity and Diversity Award from the Ontario Trillium Foundation, and I told the community activists that "given the constant vilification this community receives, it is a most noteworthy award and one of which this community should be most proud. Yes, there is a lot of talk about crime in the area, but I would wager that a comparable amount of crime occurs on Bay Street. Of course, 'white collar' crimes are considered 'indiscretions.'"

For Black youth, the system was set up in such a way as to make them feel bad about themselves, as outsiders who didn't even deserve the benefits bestowed on others in society. So I made sure to tell people at community meetings that I, personally, was very proud to be an immigrant even though I, too, had faced discrimination all along the way.

I told them that when I arrived in Canada as a student, my Dutch lab partner was allowed immigrant status in his second year, thereby allowing him access to all of the grants, bursaries, fellowships, and privileges of a landed immigrant. But I was told that I had to return to Jamaica, and that if I even so much as applied for residency, I would be deported within twenty-four hours.

It was okay, I said, to feel resentment against this white garrison-like mentality we too often ran into in Canada. I would quote these lines from "Desiderata," which should be the mantra of all immigrants: "You are a child of the universe. No less than the trees and the stars, you have a right to be here."

Because we do, absolutely, have a right to be here.

I told them they had not only a moral right but an economic right to be in Canada. In my case, I explained that, over the centuries, incredible British fortunes had been made on the Jamaican sugar trade with terribly exploited or outright slave labour. Canadian multinationals like Alcan had been digging up Jamaican bauxite for decades and shipping it through the Panama Canal to Kitimat, B.C., for processing. Canadian banks and insurance companies have dominated many parts of the Caribbean for more than a century now, draining our islands and people of capital.

Yes, we have a moral and fiduciary right to be here. Products such as sugar, rum, coffee, bananas, and spices are purchased for little or nothing with prices set in the Chicago commodity exchange.

If there existed a true partnership, a fair market value would be offered for these products, plus value added at source, thus strengthening the economies of these so-called third-world countries, thereby drastically reducing if not eliminating the need for immigration.

Blacks have made a substantial and unacknowledged contribution to the betterment of this country, and the standard of living enjoyed by its citizens. A partnership must be forged whereby our brothers and sisters may not only contribute to the wellbeing of society, but also enjoy its benefits as full participants.

I spoke these words at the close of the last century, but unfortunately they apply today to an even greater extent. The injustices are not only the same, they are increasing.

While our share of the pie was always very thin, Blacks were expected to make sacrifices along with other Canadians. This discrepancy — sacrifices without the benefits — hit home in 2002 when I was asked to give a speech at the wake for a twenty-five-year-old Black kid, Ainsworth Dyer. Born in Montreal and raised in Toronto, Dyer was one of four Canadian soldiers killed by U.S. forces during the Tarnak Farm friendly fire incident near Kandahar, Afghanistan, when the Canadians were bombed by their American allies. Corporal Ainsworth Dyer and his comrades were the first of Canada's military dead in the Afghanistan war.

Canada, I said, seemed to be in Afghanistan because after 9/11 the U.S. had warned "you are either with us or you are with the terrorists." But we had the right to be "neither with the United States nor against the United States. One can have a mind of one's own. And having endured the ravages of slavery and suppression for hundreds of years, we know from experience that one person's terrorist is another person's freedom fighter."

FLOW became a strong voice in this battle for social justice. The culture of the station was laced with the sense of commitment to the community that we had brought over from *Contrast*. FLOW had a staff of fifty-eight now, which included every race and more than a dozen nationalities. At a time when "diversity" in Toronto was generally honoured only in the abstract, at FLOW we were consciously living it day to day with a staff that included, along with Blacks, Asians, South Asians, people of Middle Eastern origins, and whites of several ethnicities. And we were still reaching our core audience. In one of the most telling statistics of our successful outreach to the Black community, a survey in the early 2000s showed that fully 100% of Toronto Blacks had heard of FLOW — and it is hard to improve on that.

The importance of FLOW to the community during this period is reflected in the response to one of our most innovative shows, *O.T.A. (On The Air) Live!* It was created and hosted by Ty Harper and Reza "rez DigitaL" Dahya and it quickly became the destination spot for weekly interviews for a Toronto hip hop community that was still vastly underrepresented on the airwaves. Both Rez and Ty were knowledgeable and charming hosts, and Ty Harper was a kind of poster child of FLOW. He told a *Vice* interviewer that his desire to work in radio began around 1990 when FLOW was in the middle of its first campaign for a station. At the time, "the only station in the Toronto area offering rap, R&B, or reggae music on public FM was Buffalo's 93.7 FM WBLK — and that was a city away." Ty said that the fact that he had to tune into a radio station in another country "was kind of just what it meant to be a Black kid in Toronto."

The first campaign by FLOW for grassroots support for the station caught his interest. He remembered "Mr. Jolly and all these guys out there knocking door to door trying to get support for this station. I was just answering the front door and when they handed us the petition I finally realized, like, 'holy shit, I want to do this.' So I literally went to school with the ambition to work for what ten years later would become FLOW."

Ty and Reza's show was described by *Vice* as "a show that managed to expand the listener's knowledge of rap music while shining a light on local talent . . . from artists like Shad, who was just coming off his first Juno nomination for his sophomore album *Old Prince*, to a young Drake who was in the midst of his first beef, mocking rapper Aristo on a call-in infomercial. More importantly, it was a space that encouraged free-flowing conversations about issues in the industry and community at large." As Dahya told *Vice*, "The heart [of the

A container of donations from Tyndall being sent to Haiti in relief efforts for Hurricane Irene in 2011.

radio] is the connection with the community, and we worked hard to keep that connection strong."

When FLOW 93.5 celebrated its fifth anniversary in 2005, we threw a party in space rented at the Royal Ontario Museum. There was a lot to celebrate. Our ratings and community support remained strong, and, on the financial side, we had surpassed our business plan. Our revenues were greater than $7 million in that fiscal year with an audience of 400,000 listeners, as well as many others streaming us over the internet.

People recognized that we were more than a business. We were the voice of a large, diverse, and dynamic community. This put us on a deeper level not only with our listeners but with local artists and even with our shareholders. I was proud of the fact that, by 2005, FLOW had already donated nearly $2 million worth of free commercial air time to worthy and charitable causes, most serving the interests of Toronto's minority communities. It was absolutely necessary for me and my team that we contributed on- and off-air resources to support community-based initiatives.

Thanks to our investment of $300,000 a year to help developing artists, we introduced about 250 new musicians to commercial radio. Our announcers and senior management team were also expected to play a role in the community. We spoke regularly at post-secondary schools and community centres. We had a comprehensive Black History Month program that we took to high schools across the Toronto area each year, backed up by our internship program to give young people an opportunity to be exposed to a commercial radio station and to receive hands-on training and experience. Each year since their launch, our FLOW Milestone Awards provided visible-minority students in Ryerson's Radio and Television Arts program with scholarship support for their tuition.

FLOW exposure helped many artists achieve record deals, including Remy Shand, Jully Black, TRD, Tef and Don, Harpoon Missile, Baby Blue Soundcrew, Sean Oliver, and India.Arie, and we were an important part of the careers of Canadian hip hop artists like Drake, Shad, Michie Mee, Maestro, Kardinal Offishall, Classified, k-os, K'naan, Swollen Members, Sweatshop Union, Buck 65, Belly, Moka Only, Kyprios, and Cadence Weapon. The station also boosted the career of CP24 reporter Nathan Downer and helped our music director, Farley Flex, get invited to serve as a judge on the first round of *Canadian Idol*.

As we had done with *Contrast*, FLOW's community mandate also included support for organizations like the Jamaican Canadian Association and the Black Business and Professional Association.

But we would still not be playing on a completely level

playing field. Even after our successes, we still ran into major advertisers who would not advertise with us because we were "too Black." In fact, they had policies of only advertising on "mainstream" stations. And they decided that Black in Canada — in their minds, still a white country — was necessarily on the margins. That has been and continues to be part of the Canadian reality and it would remain a reality for the station, somewhat stunting our growth.

We were often made to feel we were outsiders. This was visibly the case when we sponsored an outdoor concert in Mississauga with a popular rapper and the police descended en masse, with a riot squad and attack dogs. Bringing Black youth together was obviously seen as a threat.

That type of incident only added to our surprise when our station was recognized by our peers across the country during that year's Canadian Music Week as the number one contemporary radio station in Canada.

After only five years, recognition as the top station in the country was an exceptional validation. I remember walking into the station around this time and seeing all of the young talent, mostly Black but embodying the full rainbow of colours, busy with the exciting and stressful tasks of putting on live radio — and experiencing momentary amazement at what we had accomplished. We had fought for the right to express ourselves, and we had won against considerable adversity. We had become part of the change we had long wanted to see. But we were still far from the promised land. And I realized with some surprise that in a few months I would be turning seventy years old.

CHAPTER FIFTEEN

SAILING AGAINST THE WIND

Perhaps because I have a background in science, I try, as much as possible, to see the world as it is, to look for the plain truth, without the decoration of wishful thinking. Some of my friends have suggested that I can be too critical of the world we live in. But in fact, I have also rejoiced at progress that we have made. Not only in Canada but around the world. I took special pleasure when I visited South Africa in the mid-2000s with Janice Williams, whom I met in 2001 and who has become a very important part of my life in every way.

As I mentioned earlier, during the 1970s and 1980s, I had sent monthly cheques to the ANC office in exile in Zambia, attended countless anti-apartheid events in Toronto, and, on more than one occasion, knocked over South African

Me and Janice Williams.

wines in the liquor store to protest any dealings at all with that country. So it was an especially rewarding feeling to be flying with Jan to visit post-apartheid South Africa.

In Johannesburg we were reminded of what South Africans had overcome. We visited the adjacent Soweto township, where so much of the bitter battle against apartheid had been fought. A turning point in the struggle had come after the Soweto massacre on June 16, 1976, when thousands of students marched from the Naledi High School to Orlando Stadium to protest the government policy that forced them

In Soweto, South Africa, 2007.

to study in Afrikaans instead of English. They were holding innocuous signs proclaiming "If we must do Afrikaans, [Prime Minister John] Vorster must do Zulu" and singing nationalist songs when the police opened fire. Twenty-three students were killed that day, and the uprising continued through the month of June, with more than 175 people killed in the streets of Soweto by the security forces. But it was the massacre of children that exposed the murderous brutality of the apartheid regime to the world — even to those who had previously tried to turn a blind eye to it — and ignited a new wave of resistance throughout South Africa.

In Soweto, Jan and I visited the place where the first child, Hector Pieterson, was gunned down by police. Then we took a stroll down Vilakazi Street, the only street in the world that has been home to two Nobel Prize winners. The houses where Nelson Mandela and Bishop Desmond Tutu lived are still standing as a testament to the height the human spirit can reach even during the greatest darkness.

While in Johannesburg, we also visited the Apartheid Museum, which traces some of the gruesome history of the struggle and illustrates something of the day-to-day reality of the system by having four separate entrances for "Black," "coloured," "Asian," and "white" visitors. In that bizarro world, the fact of Jan and I together as a couple would have been made physically impossible in public and criminal in private. That was the sickness of that time and place and one that must never be forgotten.

During our visit to Cape Town, we saw something of the challenges still ahead. At our hotel, we met Linda Plaatijies, who worked in the hotel dining room, and Dominic Katete, who worked at the café bar. On his day off, Dominic, who had immigrated to South Africa a few years earlier from the Democratic Republic of the Congo, took us for a tour off the beaten path in the surrounding townships, like Gugulethu, where we got a firsthand sense of the financial hardship — the crowded rusty sheet-metal shacks that so many South Africans still endured, including Linda, who was the single mother of an eight-year-old daughter, Palesa.

It was important for me to see firsthand that, even after the scourge of apartheid was beaten, the rebuilding was far from over. Inequalities of wealth had been built on the injustices, with Blacks used as cheap and very expendable labour. These inequalities persist, and they are a lesson for us in North America about the complexities of levelling the playing field. Long after apartheid is gone, two white South

African businessmen, luxury goods seller Johann Rupert and Nicky Oppenheimer of De Beers, have a combined worth equal to that of the poorer half of the nation's 52 million people. Even fifteen years after apartheid ended, grinding poverty was still the rule rather than the exception for the Black majority.

The South African trip ended with a visit to a game reserve in the northeast, not far from the border with Mozambique. This was the flip side to the grinding poverty of the townships. We were staying at the Ulusaba Lodge, owned by Sir Richard Branson, whose parents happened to be staying there. I had met Richard Branson in Toronto when he stopped by the station for an interview about his cellular telephone service, Virgin Mobile, and I had been struck by his accessibility. The billionaire entrepreneur showed up at the station alone, wearing a sweatshirt, and didn't need advice on where his limo driver could park because he had taken the subway from his hotel to the station. I was especially impressed because it was not unusual for music industry types to arrive glittering with gold and jewels with an entourage of five or six managers and hangers on. But Branson sauntered in, said hello to everyone, and then got down to business in the studio delivering the message he wanted to deliver, then left with a friendly smile and wave. His parents had the same easygoing charm, and Ulusaba Lodge was a beautiful refuge.

While I enjoyed visiting Africa at both ends of the scale, I was never naive about the place and its problems. I knew that for all of its beauty and human potential, the colonial legacy has left a series of haphazardly constructed countries that, like Jamaica, were shaped almost entirely by outside interests and designed to serve outside needs.

I had already seen the results of this during a trip to Kenya in the 1980s. I had gone as part of a tour group, but I left the group in Nairobi and rented a car to drive down to the coastal city Mombasa.

It turned out to be an eventful trip. I had car trouble on the way to Mombasa, and I had to wait at a roadside stop for the rental company to send a replacement. I learned a bit about African informality when I ordered lunch in a small cantina and the very pleasant waitress not only sat with me and chatted but helped herself to some of my food.

Mombasa was a beautiful tropical city on the Indian ocean with a lively nightlife. But it was also a distinctly Muslim town with the daily call to prayer blasting through loudspeakers. This only added to the sense of the exotic, the magic of legendary places that you often find in Africa.

Before returning to Nairobi, I took a side trip up the coast to Lamu Island, where the 1,200-year-old Lamu Town is recognized as the oldest continually inhabited town in East Africa. It is also the best preserved, and the only car on the whole island belongs to the governor. It was a stunningly beautiful place with the dhows pulled up on the beaches and the originally Swahili architecture making you feel you could be back in the fourteenth century with artisans and other sellers operating out of what we in Jamaica called *bend down plazas*, where goods are simply laid out on the ground. Unfortunately, I could not eat in

Lamu because of stomach problems, so I was also happy to discover there was a drugstore in the town. The pharmacist showed me all of the Western medicines on one side of the store and the traditional medicines on the other. I asked to try the traditional and, for what it's worth, it worked within minutes in relieving what had been a serious stomach upset.

When I arrived back in Mombasa, it was already time for me to return to Nairobi for my flight. I was late getting away and faced driving most of the eight-hour trip over rough roads at night. Something told me that it wasn't safe to do this, so I arranged for a driver to take me and the rental car to Nairobi and I would pay his way back. As it turned out, it was a wise move. In the middle of nowhere, around midnight, I was dozing off when I was jolted awake by the sound of two of our tires blowing. The driver said we had hit a spiked strip that bandits laid across the road to stop cars at night and asked if I minded if we just kept driving on the rims rather than stop on the side of the road where we would likely find ourselves surrounded by armed thieves. I of course encouraged him to keep driving and to hell with the rims.

When we reached a town with a mechanic who would sell us new rims and tires, the driver said to him, "Look, we're businessmen from Nairobi and we're armed so don't fuck with us."

That is how the world works in the hinterlands that have been stripped of their wealth by the colonial and then neo-colonial powers. In Africa, and in other formerly colonial countries like Jamaica, you will meet the warmest and most generous people in the world; but on the edges, desperation reigns.

Me and Governor General of Canada Michaëlle Jean, 2009.

At home in Canada in the mid-2000s, there were signs of positive change, at least at the symbolic level. In 2005, Michaëlle Jean was appointed Canada's twenty-seventh Governor General by Prime Minister Paul Martin. She was an unexpected choice, not only as a Black woman but as a Caribbean-born woman from a family that had fled the Duvalier dictatorship in Haiti. Her appointment was at first well received, but the old Canada seemed to briefly flare up when she was variously attacked as a Quebec separatist and then as a French citizen plant in the midst of Canada. Many of us suspected it was not really about separatism or about the citizenship she had acquired in marriage to her husband that were causing these unprecedented attacks on a newly appointed Governor General. Yet it was Jean's own intelligence and grace, and her commitment to the young and to Indigenous peoples in the country, that eventually won Canadians over. I was very happy to have the honour of meeting her when we shared a table at the Harry Jerome event.

Then, in 2008, Barack Obama won what for many was an astounding victory in the United States presidential election, something most of us thought was impossible. For Black Canadians, the real symbolism of these two events hit home in February 2009 when Obama made his first visit to Canada and was met at the air force base in Ottawa by Michaëlle Jean. You would have to have a very hard heart not to be affected by the two leaders as they walked the red carpet to the waiting cars: a Black man and a Black woman as heads of states of the two white North American countries.

Unfortunately, you would also have to be very naive if you thought that this meant that we had suddenly made a great leap forward to the post-racial world simply by changing, temporarily, the personnel at the top.

This idea that Canadians are not racist is one that we like to entertain as we congratulate ourselves over our diversity. For example, after Karīm al-Hussainī, the 49th Aga Khan of the Ismaili Muslims, described Canada as "the most successful pluralist society on the face of our globe" and "a model for the world," he was rewarded by being made an honorary citizen of the country.

But at the same moment that the Aga Khan was saying these things, a Nova Scotia convenience store security camera was recording two police officers beating up nineteen-year-old Brendan Clarke. The Black teenager had gone to buy chewing gum, and he tried to pay with a $100 bill. The person at the counter called the police. The bill was legitimate, but this did not deter the police from beating up Brendan and then arresting him for resisting arrest, causing a disturbance, and assaulting a police officer. Most of the battering took place on the store's surveillance camera, but the cops deliberately moved Brendan away from the coverage area of the camera while punching and manhandling him. The victim of police violence was convicted on the charge of disturbing the peace, until the video surfaced and all charges against him were then thrown out. That is part of the reality of Black Canadians.

The facts on the ground revealed that Brendan's Canada was more true to life than the Aga Khan's when the *Toronto Star* published the findings of its landmark investigation into police racial profiling in Toronto. It obtained access to police data that recorded 480,000 incidents of police contact with civilians from 1996 to 2001 that generated a ticket or arrest. It was clearly established that Blacks received far different treatment from the police.

Of those taken to the station, Blacks were held behind bars for a court appearance 15.5% of the time, more than twice the rate of whites. The *Toronto Star*'s investigation also uncovered the existence of the "DWB" or "Driving While Black" phenomenon, whereby Blacks were disproportionately charged for on-site offences such as failing to update a driver's licence or driving without insurance. As the newspaper pointed out, "Police discover such violations only after a motorist has been pulled over. And in the absence of any other charge, it isn't clear why drivers involved in these offences are stopped in the first place."

When the same survey was conducted eight years later, in March 2010, it found that the situation had not improved — in fact it had gotten worse, especially with the carding practice, whereby police stop people on the streets and take down their personal information.

The *Toronto Star* report found that "while blacks make up 8.3 per cent of Toronto's population, they accounted for 25 per cent of the cards filled out between 2008 and mid-2011," a rate now three times as high as whites. The report found that Blacks were more likely than whites to be stopped and carded in every one of the city's patrol zones. Most tellingly, "the likelihood increases in areas that are predominantly white."

It is important to look at the facts when trying to measure our progress. We absolutely should recognize and celebrate when we make advances as a society but we must also recognize that progress is uneven. In some basic areas, like justice on the streets of Toronto, we were going backward, not forward, in the first decade of the new millennium.

We have a clear example of this in the ever-wavering fortunes of our most significant success: Caribana. While we were celebrating the fifth anniversary of FLOW, Caribana was teetering due to its continuous underfunding by governments. At the time, it was bringing $300 million into the Toronto economy. (It now brings more than half a billion dollars a year.) Yet Eurocentric politicians, year after year, begrudged any subsidy at all to this celebration of Caribbean-Canadian culture. Tons of cash is handed over to the Art Gallery of Ontario, and to the National Ballet, which generates 1/84th the amount of economic activity that Caribana brings to the city. But government support to Caribana remains minuscule compared to what is given to the ballet company.

The situation was becoming dire for Caribana in the mid-2000s. The festival was on the verge of collapse due to a $200,000 Revenue Canada bill that sucked up all of its working capital. It had already reached the point where the office fax machines were being repossessed when I formed a committee with Carl Masters and Romain Pitt to raise funds to pay off the festival's debts. We did raise a considerable amount of money, and the funds were given to Charles Roach to deal with debtors. But we quickly ran into another problem. And this one could be pinned on certain elements within our own community.

None of us who had come to the rescue were Trinidadians, and while we were working hard to keep the festival afloat, some of the Trinidadians running the show refused to be up front with us. At one point, the management group had given us the impression they were still waiting for a government subsidy when it had already arrived, and at another, after we worked long into the night over a new business plan, we learned that part of the management group had secretly submitted its own business plan to the government without telling us. I blasted them, telling them that Caribana was a sacred trust that belonged to the whole community and they had no right to handle it so cavalierly.

Then I stepped back from the whole thing.

The real problem remained that the government was dramatically underfunding the festival, but the sectarianism in our community was certainly a complicating factor. Eventually the festival was taken out of the hands of that group and put under the influence of its major sponsor. Caribana was rechristened the Scotiabank Toronto Caribbean Carnival, but by 2016 Scotiabank had also pulled out. The scramble continues to find support for what is by every measure the greatest cultural event in the city.

As Blacks, we have to use every resource we have to protect not only our fragile institutions, but even our fundamental rights. One tool that gained a new effectiveness during the new millennium is the vote. Our numbers have continued to grow, and with hundreds of thousands of Blacks in Toronto, we have reached the point where we recognize that if we stand together, we can force real change on the city and make a real difference in the province and even the country.

To help marshal our forces, a group of us — headed by Jamaican-born businesswoman Delores Lawrence, and including Hamlin Grange, former CBC producer Cynthia Reyes, and Bromley Armstrong — launched Operation Black Vote Canada "to educate, motivate, and inspire members of Canada's black community (adults and youths) to participate in the political process at all levels, especially voting."

We believed that if we could empower young people by getting them involved in the democratic process — even through something as basic as going out to vote — they would not only feel that they were part of the system but actually be able to vote together to try to change it. As Delores Lawrence put it at our first meeting in 2005, "Generations of young Blacks could be lost to crime, poverty, and despair if their community fails to mobilize politically. We as a people have to stop doing lip service to the social problems that plague us. We have to be involved."

For older Blacks, the issue was often even more basic. They had been so long frozen out from mainstream society that many had not even gotten their Canadian citizenship. Reaching out and helping them get citizenship was another of our priorities.

But we also acknowledged it was a two-way street. While it was important to get our people into the political process, it was also important to ensure that the political process valued our contributions. We lobbied to have Blacks appointed to positions in the 600 agencies, boards, and commissions within the Province of Ontario from which they had been excluded, and held information sessions for community members that showed how they could put their names forward.

Unfortunately, this wasn't getting any easier in the new millennium. Young Blacks were not only still being shunted aside and left behind, they were still being beaten and shot by police in depressingly large numbers. Where the improvement came was that with the increase of surveillance and cellphone cameras, it was easier to catch abusive police officers in action.

While this police discrimination was going on, an even more damaging hysteria was being promoted by the press, which began running ominous stories of Black street gangs and attributing much of the violence in the city to Blacks. The reality was that most of the Blacks involved in the drug trade were young people who had been hired and armed by either the Hells Angels or the Italian Mafia and used as mercenaries by the established crime groups. Cynthia Reyes, with whom I was working in Operation Black Vote, referred to a recent CBC piece that had revealed the Hells Angels and Mafia connection to the Black drug trade in a note she sent to the Operation Black Vote committee: "These Black and South Asian kids are the ones getting killed or doing the killing, but it's white men who are selling them guns illegally and white men who are their bosses."

That was the type of double standard we faced. While the media was constantly demanding that the "Black community" get its act together to prevent the shootings and the drug trade they were part of, we wondered why no one was demanding that the Italian community get its act together to get rid of the Mafia that was calling the shots in the industry. "Why," Reyes asked, "is nobody asking what is being done to catch the white bosses or suppliers?"

The question became even more pertinent in 2011, when gun violence reached even into our high schools. That was the year that fifteen-year-old Jordan Manners was found gasping for breath from what turned out to be a fatal gunshot wound in a hallway of Jane-Finch's C.W. Jefferys Collegiate. That is how things progressed in Toronto: from police violence to what is now referred to as lateral violence. Since the still-unsolved murder of Jordan Manners, more than a dozen youth under nineteen years old have been murdered in the neighbourhood; in 2013, this orgy of killing resulted in the murder of four friends — three fifteen-year-olds and one sixteen-year-old — within blocks of each other in separate incidents, making the neighbourhood far and away the most dangerous place to be a kid in Canada.

One of the things FLOW allowed us to do during this period was to counter the stereotypes of Black youth as violent gang members — the image presented in mainstream media. We also identified our station with positive images in the Black community like having a float in every Caribana parade and promoting it on our station. We used our voice to fight back against the violence in the streets and also the violence of the mainstream media imagery that was painting our community as the cause of all of society's ills.

The drug trade was eating away at the fabric of Toronto, no doubt, but the real perpetrators were not the people in Jane-Finch struggling to survive. Young Blacks were, at almost every turn, the first victims in this Mafia- and biker-controlled industry as the violent trade was ignited in their neighbourhoods. At least on our radio station, we were able to give the other side of the story: a Black community that was not at all the cause of the plague, but its greatest victim.

FLOW managed to stay at the centre of things all through this period. As president and CEO, I was kept up to date on the day-to-day issues, and I continued spending an enormous amount of time at the station meeting with Nicole, who was then serving as station manager; program director Wayne Williams; advertising director Byron Garby; and all of the other key personnel. All were dedicated and hard-working, but it was easy to get overwhelmed by the sheer weight of detail it takes to run a twenty-four-hour news and entertainment broadcaster. The challenge was always internal communications, ensuring everyone knew at all times what everyone else was doing.

The pace, as it always is with live radio, was frenetic. In commercial radio, the show is loaded into the computer by the music director before they go on air so the music and scripted parts flow together, while the traffic person inserts commercials and imaging bits; the DJ has to be nimble enough to move back and forth between the music, commercials, sound effects, scripts, improvised comments, and interviews with live guests, while the news person is on the phone or rewriting wire copy and collecting sound for the twice-an-hour newscast. The web person is continually hovering around picking up scripts and clips for updating to the web, and the promotions department is buzzing in and out with five or six kids who are ferried around town in two or three vehicles to work at presentations or street giveaways. And, of course, the advertising staff is manning the phones to sweet-talk existing clients to try to get them to renew or expand their presence or beating the bushes to find new ones.

During all this time, the mainly Black artists are arriving and leaving for interviews or simply hanging out, adding a sense of excitement. The celebrity guests often created a stir. One of them, Kanye West, didn't stay long — he stormed out of the interview when he was told he could not refer to women as "bitches" on air.

As you can imagine, glitches and all manner of screw-ups occurred frequently amid the controlled chaos, and my days were generally spent trouble shooting. Equipment issues were not uncommon. Through an antenna specially constructed in Italy, our signals went to First Canadian Place, where we rented the space, and we needed a full-time engineer on staff to ensure that any signal problems were quickly dealt with.

There were also endless regulatory issues to be addressed and different fees we had to pay to the CRTC and to royalty funds for musicians. This added to the already complicated budgeting process as the managers not only had to oversee the spending of regular operations but ensure that all our payments were up to date, as well as our receivables from our advertisers, who were notoriously slow in cutting cheques. It was so complicated, in fact, that one of our accountants managed to skim $400,000 from us over time simply by taking deposits to the bank and pocketing the small cash portion. When we discovered the discrepancy and the extent of the theft, we had a decision to make. If we called the police on the guy, that would be that, the money would be gone. Instead, we confronted the employee and demanded he return the money or the police would be called in. The thieving employee took the offer, mortgaged his house, and repaid.

To add to the confusion, we often did live broadcasts from one of the Toronto clubs, or our promotions department would hire a first-rate Canadian band and put on a promotional event — a party, in fact — to back a cause or simply to promote our brand. So, the station was never nine to five. I would sometimes spend the morning there, the afternoon at the Tyndall residence out in Mississauga, then be back at the end of the day for a management team meeting, and be out that night at a FLOW event to give a welcoming speech and touch base with industry people. During those off-site broadcasts, all bets were off, with an infinite possibly for mishaps. No matter what you did in studio or off-site, one thing was sure: a certain percentage of your audience would be shocked and appalled, and they would let you know it.

It was an exciting but exhausting period. I had quite a lot of personal visibility in Toronto at the time, to the point where I was given the City Soul Award by the Canadian Urban Institute. I was also invited to the House of Commons for the Black History Month celebration, acknowledged from the floor by one of the Liberal members, and invited to a reception afterward that was hosted by then–Prime Minister Paul Martin.

But the fact was I was gritting my teeth to keep smiling during this period because I was suffering from excruciating lower back pain. I kept going because I really didn't have time to be out of commission.

Among other external activities, I was invited onto the board of the Toronto International Film Festival, but I admit I was unimpressed by the experience. The board members tended to come from the high-snob end of Toronto, and I don't think in the three years that I was there anyone actually asked my opinion of anything. Around this time, I was also on the board of the YMCA and the city's economic development council, and these were much more positive experiences working with people who believed in a cause, rather than the TIFFers who tended to be more in search of the reflected glory and glamour of the film festival.

But the back pain was getting the better of me. Finally, in 2008, and again in 2009, I went into Sunnybrook Hospital for major back surgery and spent many weeks out of commission in rehab at Lyndhurst learning to walk again. Difficult times — but I was fortunate to have Jan to help me get through this. She encouraged me at literally every step of the way and that kind of support is appreciated more than I can ever say.

Even through these trials, the radio station, by almost every measure, was continuing to perform at a high level. But what was changing, slowly at first and then with a dramatic jolt, was the industry ecology.

Already by 2006, there were indications that the ground was shifting when industry ad revenues began falling. We were healthy enough that we could make adjustments to keep ourselves in the black; but by 2006, when FLOW had its licence renewed for another seven years, there were rumours of coming mergers in what was already a highly competitive industry, as the big players sought to establish even greater dominance.

The first quake hit in 2007 when the Slaights sold Standard Radio to Harold Greenberg's production house, Astral Media. Astral had made its money on pay TV channels and the softcore *Porky's* movie series and then had gone big into cable TV stations. To expand into the radio industry, the Greenbergs paid a then-astounding $1.08 billion for Standard, a company that the Slaights had bought from Conrad Black in 1987 for $180 million.

During this period, we were also in a good position to sell FLOW at that sort of astronomical profit, but we had not spent a dozen years and all of that blood, sweat, and tears to cash in at the first opportunity. We decided to hold on, and it is a testament to his belief in the special FLOW mission that Gary Slaight also kept his share in our station and protected us from becoming part of the Astral empire. He understood that we were more than a business, and I think he believed in our cause of giving voice and opportunity to the voiceless and sidelined people in Toronto.

Even as CEO of one of the most powerful broadcasting companies in the country, Gary remembered that he had started out in a family that could barely pay the bills while living over a store in Edmonton. He knew what it was like to be the little guy. When he became the city's newest billionaire with the sale of his company to Astral, he showed what he was made of. He has become almost legendary in Toronto for his generosity, giving millions to SickKids, War Child, the Stephen Lewis Foundation, and many other worthy causes, and acting as the white knight for arts organizations in Toronto like Luminato and the Soulpepper Theatre Company.

As it turned out, the Standard-to-Astral deal was only part of the merger mania in the broadcasting industry. CHUM Ltd. was then swallowed up by Bell Globemedia, when CHUM not only controlled thirty-three radio stations but held full or joint control of two Canadian television systems — Citytv and A-Channel (formerly NewNet, now CTV Two) — comprising eleven local stations and one CBC Television affiliate, one provincial educational channel, and twenty branded specialty television channels, most notably MuchMusic and its various spinoffs.

Bell Globemedia (soon to become Bell Media) was owner of the CTV Television Network, although the CRTC required CHUM Ltd. to sell off five of its television stations to Rogers. The new Bell Media company instantly became a broadcasting powerhouse and, thanks to CHUM, a giant in the radio industry.

For FLOW, this sale had immediate ramifications. We had been partnered with CHUM in Edmonton, and the sale meant that we were now partners with Bell Media in that market.

While the media mergers shook the ground around us, we continued to watch ad rates sink as the new conglomerates were able to further cut rates. To counter this, Nicole designed an ad campaign around a "New FLOW," which really wasn't anything different except a new packaging for ad sales. It had its desired and one undesired effect: on the desired side, it did boost our market share; but on the undesired side, it caused some of our community members to question our commitment to our mission. I say "community members" and not "listeners" because listeners would have heard no change in content from one day to the other — the New FLOW was about new packaging for the advertisers. But, once again, we had to assure the community that FLOW was still a Black-run station.

One of the issues that we worried about unnecessarily was the arrival of Sirius Satellite Radio. The whole industry panicked with the idea that our radio market was suddenly expanded from citywide to worldwide, and we wrung our hands at the thought of being in competition with the stations in New York and L.A., as well as all of the other Toronto stations. But that turned out to be a false alarm. Radio, we should have known, is decidedly local, like the daily newspaper. There is room for the odd national station like the CBC, but even they must have a robust local component to survive. For the most part, people turn on the radio to hear what is happening where they live, and this was especially the case for our listeners.

Sirius would not be a problem. But the market was not staying still. It was continuing to evolve in the wrong direction. As the new giants in the industry restructured, they were able to dramatically increase their economies of scale. Suddenly, only one music director was needed to program five stations, and three stations would share a single general manager. Employment costs dropped dramatically, and in radio the overwhelming cost is in salaries. This meant big players were able to offer multi-city deals to their advertisers at significantly reduced ad rates.

We continued through 2008 and 2009, fighting the battle and cutting our costs to the minimum to stay out of the red, but by 2010 the writing was on the wall. Ad rates had fallen to a third of what they had been when we started, and even the book value of the station had dropped by about half. The market was speaking loud and clear. Even though our listenership was moving up, with a more than 25% increase in our market share, the new ever-falling pricing structure no longer allowed for a stand-alone station. That was the reality. The board discussed options. The only way we could compete with the new monster companies was if we dramatically cut costs, and that meant both losing personnel and slashing salaries of the remaining staff to match the falling revenue base. But that would significantly reduce the quality of the station, which would soon be reflected in declining listenership, which of course would further reduce ad revenues. It would be a downward spiral and we could see no way forward.

CHAPTER SIXTEEN

ESSE NON VIDERI — TO BE, AND NOT TO SEEM

The industry knew the station was vulnerable. Approaches were made from all sides. The thought of selling FLOW to one of the broadcasting giants was difficult to consider. But it also seemed inescapable. All of us on the board felt the station still had a role to play; we also knew that in our decade at the helm, we had helped to dramatically change the broadcast market in Toronto and had been an important part of the movement forward of our community. The airwaves now had a core of seasoned Black professionals on both sides of the microphone that had gotten a start and honed their talents working for FLOW. Black music was now everywhere on the Toronto airwaves and this, too, tended to reduce the necessity of a Black-owned station. Our voices were being heard. Not near as loud as we would have liked, but at least to a greater degree than ever before.

When a serious offer came from Bell Media through its CTV subsidiary, we had to listen. And then things moved with incredible speed. Carolyn Stamegna, the media lawyer who had coached us with our bid in 1998, was there to work out the sale. The terms would be half of what they would have been a few years earlier because the precipitous fall in radio industry revenues meant individual stations were worth less than they had been. We had stood our ground as long as we could.

We came to an agreement in late 2010. On December 23, the CRTC approved the deal in principle for the sale of "the assets of CFXJ-FM (known as *The New Flow 93.5*)" to Bell Media; and at the same time, we negotiated the sale of our 49% interest in the Edmonton Urban station we owned with CHUM to Rogers. For a station that had taken more than a decade to build, the end came at a dizzying speed.

All that was left was the final hand-off. CTV took ownership of 93.5 FLOW in February 2011 with their radio division president, Chris Gordon, saying the company was committed keeping the station "very rhythmic." In approving the sale, the company was bound through 2017 to the terms of FLOW's original licence, which was for the operation of an urban music format.

With the ownership transfer, the studios and offices moved from 211 Yonge Street to CTV's 299 Queen Street facility, where CHUM AM and FM were located. The personnel changes came quickly. My daughter Nicole resigned from her post when the transfer was made, and thirty-four of fifty-eight employees were gradually given buyout packages. Among those departing were program director Wayne Williams and virtually all of the on-air personalities. The vice president of sales, Byron Garby, remained with the company, as did two of his six sales reps. The most important element of continuity was that music director Justin Dumont was kept on. Many of the team would be missed. Not only by listeners but by artists. Drake gave a Facebook shout out to Ty Harper and Reza Dahya for their work on FLOW, and I was happy to hear later that both men continued making their mark, with Reza making films and Ty working at CBC with Shad, who had taken over from Jian Ghomeshi at *q*. We have made a continuing impact. Even today when I checked *Billboard Magazine*, three of the six Canadians on the Top 100 are urban artists from Toronto: Drake, The Weeknd, and Tory Lanez.

It was an important wrapping-up era for me. At the same time that the sale of FLOW was going through, I was also selling the nursing home business that I had started forty years earlier when I was still teaching chemistry and physics at Forest Hill. The nursing home, which I had built into a 260-bed complex on 2.5 acres that included a retirement home, had been for sale for two years, but after I waited out the circling sharks, the right buyer with the right price appeared and the deal was done.

It was time.

I was seventy-five years old and I was ready to step

back from the work-a-day world that I had entered in 1953 when I had arrived at the West Indies Sugar Company plantation gates fresh out of Cornwall College. Since then, I had put in almost sixty years as a clerk, technician, teacher, businessman, publisher, and broadcaster. There were still other business interests that I had to look after, but there were also other things I wanted to do. Maybe travel a bit more with Jan and help out more with some non-profit organizations that I was involved with. It was time for stepping back, but not at all for stepping out.

In fact, I could not step out. I continued to speak out and support our activist organizations and many of our political voices, people I admire for going into that difficult life. I had in years past been sounded out more than once by more than one political party about running under their banner, but that was not for me. I knew I would not be able to do it well because it is not in my nature to accept party discipline and stay silent when I have something to say, or to say something I do not truly believe in, which you have to be willing to do in party politics. It is more my nature to picket my own organization — like I did with the BBPA when Prime Minister Mulroney was speaking at the gala — than to accept remaining silent about something that bothers me. My politics are more direct. I speak to people face to face, generally to community groups and to activists, and what has always concerned me most are attacks on the young. Today, the flashpoint is the carding issue.

In one form or another, "carding" has been going

on forever. It is a form of racial profiling where police randomly stop people, question them about their activities and even their friends, ask for identification, and then put that information in their database. It is questionable whether this practice is even legal, but what is certain is that anyone who has not given the police a legitimate reason for official interest has the right to walk away without answering. The police, however, do not make this apparent. They often carry out their carding in groups of two or three and surround the person they are stopping so they are, as one civil rights lawyer put it, "psychologically detained" while they are being questioned.

Not only does this practice violate basic civil liberties, it is far from random. Young Black men are far more likely to be carded than any other group. This blatant form of racism is disturbing in itself, but in too many cases it leads to real and immediate consequences when young Blacks refuse to comply. One thing many studies have shown — and we have known all along — is that there is a much more severe response when a Black man does not comply with a police request than a white man; in their dealings with Blacks, police are far more likely to escalate a conflict than to try to defuse it. And this is a recipe for disaster.

The dangerous collision happens when a young Black man, having already been illegally detained on the street in numerous humiliating stops, finally refuses to listen to the police. The first response of the police, even though the young man has every right to ignore them, is to escalate. Encircle him, challenge him. And if he does not submit — and I use the word in the literal sense of *show submission*

— to the white officer, he will very likely be prodded and provoked into an action that allows them to immediately manhandle and arrest him. If he breaks free, guns are drawn.

That is how it plays out over and over again throughout North America. And each year, the young Black victims of this racial profiling became angrier and angrier at their treatment, and the police respond by becoming more and more aggressive in their carding practices. In the U.S. today, the police killing spree of young Blacks has reached astounding proportions, and Canada is not immune. As I write this, the past two weeks have brought news of another police killing in the beating to death of Abdirahman Abdi by the Ottawa police. Three days later, Toronto police officer James Forcillo was sentenced to six years in prison, having been found guilty of attempted murder in the fatal shooting of Sammy Yatim on an empty streetcar in July 2013. In the U.S. and now in Canada, young people are fighting back with the Black Lives Matter movement, and it is important that we support them in every way.

Because of the very real danger it poses to minority youth, we have been fighting carding as a community. I signed a petition condemning carding along with some of Toronto's Black activists — Zanana Akande, Jean Augustine, Mary Anne Chambers, and Alvin Curling, the former speaker of the Ontario Legislative Assembly and co-author of the *Roots of Youth Violence Report* — as well as some of the progressive luminaries of white Toronto, including former mayors David Crombie and Barbara Hall, former Ontario justice minister Roy McMurtry, Stephen Lewis, and Michele Landsberg.

In the petition, we stated that carding did not fit the vision of a "Toronto that is inclusive, diverse, welcoming, and respectful." Collectively, we said we were "offended by the notion of casually and routinely stopping citizens, outside of police investigations of actual criminal acts, to question and record and then store personal data in police files. We are deeply distressed that Toronto residents of colour are subjected to this invasion of their privacy when the overwhelming majority of white-skinned citizens are not."

Carding was a major issue in the 2014 Toronto municipal elections, which pitted the right-wing Ford brothers (first Rob, then, when he became ill mid-campaign, his brother Doug) against the more moderate conservative John Tory and the former NDP MP Olivia Chow. Of the three, Olivia Chow was the most energetic in her opposition to carding but when she slipped to third in the polls, some members of the Black community lobbied for us to vote en masse for John Tory, who seemed to have been brought around on the carding issue to the point where he was also promising to end the practice. So, with the looming alternative of one of the Ford brothers, most Blacks in Toronto got behind John Tory, and I was convinced to add my name to those publicly supporting him in the last days before the vote.

But our community was clearly betrayed. Within six months of the election, the new mayor had abandoned his promise to end carding in the face of police chief Bill Blair's refusal to implement the policy. Tory appointed a retired judge to "mediate" and the result was that with very little change, the police carding policy was back.

Shortly after this about-face, I was invited to speak at a memorial luncheon for Dudley Laws, who to my mind remains the social, moral, and legal compass of our community — he was never afraid to speak truth to power, no matter what the consequences. I couldn't resist pointing out that "if Dudley Laws was active today, he would still be fighting against the pernicious practice by the Metropolitan Police Service of carding, where young Blacks are stopped and questioned for no reason, and then entered into their database with the life-destructive marker of 'known to police.'

"The Toronto Police Services board approved and endorsed a policy of racial profiling — carding — to keep track of residents who look like me . . . From now on, any Toronto police officer can arbitrarily stop me without informing me of my rights, when no offence has been committed . . . As the *Star*'s Shawn Micallef put it, it is a civic relationship that is 'warped, wrong, and racist.'"

I concluded by saying it's too bad we do not have a recall legislation in Canada to kick out duplicitous politicians like Tory.

In response to the community's continuing activism against carding, the provincial Liberal government has said it would move to eliminate the practice, but at this writing it remains in force. And our young Black men are still put into what can be, literally, mortal danger from the police who now turn up more and more often at Black community events under the guise of community policing. Things have not gotten better.

To the white reader, I have to stress again that for Black people these basic and continuing infringements of our rights are not abstractions and they are not mere distractions. They remain part of our day-to-day reality and cast a long dark shadow over it.

I will give you example of the "Driving While Black" offence, a form of racial profiling that has been part of my experience of Canadian life from the beginning. I have been stopped and ticketed for infractions I didn't even know existed. For inadvertently squealing my tires on hot melting pavement in summer and for having my old insurance certificate in the car along with the new one. One of my most blatant Driving While Black offences occurred back in the 1980s when I was driving to a nursing home conference in Orillia in my new Ford wagon. I was a bit early, so I pulled into a gas station down the street from the conference hall to fill up before heading inside.

I was inside listening to the opening remarks when I noticed two burly OPP officers enter from the back and begin to urgently scan the room. I had a sinking feeling. And sure enough, when they saw my Black face, they swaggered over in my direction.

They gruffly told me to follow them outside, and I had to face the humiliation of being led out of the conference. Once outside, they checked my ID and my car ownership and radioed it all in. Apparently, the gas station attendant had thought there was something so suspicious about a Black man driving a new car that he called the police. When the OPP officers located the car in the parking lot, public safety demanded that they drag me out of the conference and put me through the check.

In case you think I am dredging up a past that no longer exists in Canada, remember the fender bender on Parliament Street that I described in the opening, when the police officer threatened to put a gun in my face to force me to comply with his order to call a tow truck. This remains the reality for Blacks in Toronto and across the country. That is why I continue to speak out when I am invited to address community groups. My message is always the same: we will never have a truly decent society unless we insist on it. We must not be shy about standing up and raising our voices. When people come to me to ask me to support them, I rarely turn them down.

As someone who has had some success in business, I am also frequently asked for more direct help, for emergency loans to pay phone bills or money for education, or more than once for funds to ship a deceased relative back to Jamaica for burial. Again, I try to help where I can. How could I not? After all, I was raised by Miss Ina, who drilled into all her children, and the many neighbour kids who frequently shared our table, the importance of helping those in need as firmly as she did the importance of good table manners. In both cases, she believed the impulses should be automatic.

In turn, I have myself been rewarded in many ways for my work on behalf of my community, and I am grateful for the honours. It would be arrogant to slough them off, because it seems to me a kind of backhanded insult to those who have bestowed them. Over the past twenty years I have been given numerous awards and I have included a list of them

Receiving the prestigious Man of Might Award at Cornwall College, my alma mater, in Montego Bay, 2015.

in an appendix. In virtually all cases, they were given not as personal recognition but to recognize a common struggle of a group of us standing up on behalf of a community that is so often pushed down. This is something I was in a position to do because as a self-employed businessman I was free to speak my mind. I was in great company with friends like Bromley Armstrong, Al Hamilton, Jean Augustine, Charles Roach, Zanana Akande, Dudley Laws, and so many more who fought for our full share of justice, and with inspiration from the previous generation like Harry Gairey and Violet

Blackman, who used Marcus Garvey as a light to guide the way for us.

Still, I must confess that the award that gave me the most sentimental pleasure was an award I received from my high school in Montego Bay in the fall of 2015.

My trip to Jamaica that September had two purposes. One was to accept an award from Cornwall College and the other was to see about the sale of the family land that my mother had signed over to me in gratitude for taking care of all of her expenses in her final years.

My ties to the college had remained through the more than sixty years since I had graduated. I sponsored a number of scholarships and made donations and, in the 1970s, even helped found a Toronto chapter of the Cornwall College Old Boys' Association, designed to support the next generation of students with scholarships and bursaries, and support the school in purchasing library material or audiovisual equipment and, more recently, computers.

Jan and I arrived at the airport in Montego Bay a few days before the ceremony at Cornwall College. Even though it has been more than fifty years since I have lived in Jamaica, the heat that greets me whenever I step out of the Montego Bay airport terminal is like a welcome home, a family embrace.

The eighty-kilometre drive to Negril, where I have a vacation house, is like a decompression chamber: it lets me readjust to Jamaica. Highway A1, which runs along the edge of the Island, is never more than a couple hundred yards from the sea. Jan and I passed the gates of the self-contained all-inclusive resorts that dot the coast — the symbol of the new Jamaica. Within forty-five minutes, we had passed the yellow-painted plaster of the 300-year-old Anglican church in Lucea, where my mother's funeral was held. From there, we continued through my family's land in Industry Cove. My father's two-story house was gone — it had burned down several years earlier — and further on, Green Island was no longer the bustling sugar port it had once been. It had settled into quiet rurality, a sleepy town between the tourist destinations of Montego Bay and Negril.

From Green Island, it is only a twenty-minute drive to my vacation home. Along a straight stretch, the government has erected stand-up pylons along the side of the highway to keep the small planes of the Caribbean drug trade from using it as a landing strip. That trade is a scourge in Jamaica as it is in all Caribbean countries within a short range of the American market.

On our arrival in Negril, we found the whole country abuzz about the visit of the British prime minister, David Cameron. He arrived with Jamaica already in the middle of a lively discussion about demanding reparations for the 200 years of free labour when the British owned slaves on the island. The proposal was actually quite modest: that the British Crown pay the equivalent of the amount paid to the British slave-owners for their "loss of human property" when slavery was abolished in the Empire. The money would go to the descendants of that "human property." In 2015, it would amount to £17 billion, or about $30 billion Canadian. A very considerable amount of the wealth amassed by the

Western world was made during those brutal and shameful centuries of slavery. Asking for the equivalent of the 1834 compensation payment was a very tiny drop in a very big bucket.

University College in London had compiled a database of the compensated slave-owners. It included ancestors of novelists George Orwell and Graham Greene, and distant relatives of Arts Council chairman Sir Peter Bazalgette and celebrity chef Ainsley Harriott. The Jamaican campaigners also called on Cameron to make a personal apology, noting that one of his own ancestors was paid compensation for the loss of slaves in 1834: General Sir James Duff, Cameron's first cousin six times removed, was awarded about £3 million in today's pounds.

But of course, Cameron refused even this symbolic gesture. In a bizarre twist, he came with £25 million to build a large prison in Jamaica where Britain could send Jamaican citizens serving sentences in the U.K., once again in chains. This was on top of the mass deportation of Jamaicans who were sent back as soon as their prison sentences were completed. Many of these, like those deported from Canada and other Western countries, had left Jamaica as children or even infants and were, in every respect, products of the societies where they were raised. Without any prospects or family support, they quickly fell into a life of crime, mainly the drug trade, and thus the Jamaican problem continued to grow as other Western governments unloaded domestically produced criminals onto the island.

In the case of Canada, many deportees were young people raised by mothers who worked as servants to wealthy

Canadians and never had a chance to get citizenship. One false step and these young people found themselves dumped into the streets of Kingston with no legal means to survive. In one case, a Toronto Jamaican was murdered within days of being sent back; I was asked to help pay to bring his body back to Canada, which was the only country he had really known.

I've always hated deportation. It is a cruel punishment that has the effect of both worsening the problem — causing increased criminality because the deportees have no source of income when they arrive in what is for them an unfamiliar country — and dumping it on someone else's doorstep. Yet the deportations continue, from Canada, the U.S., and the U.K. — dozens and even hundreds of people, generally young men with no prospects, being thrown onto the streets of Kingston or Montego Bay. In these matters, the British, the Americans and, yes, the Canadians are shameless.

The Jamaican government, of course, is far from perfect. It did not press the British hard enough for compensation — or even acknowledgement of the huge sums in raw human labour they stole over the centuries of slavery. Jamaican governments since the defeat of the first coming of Michael Manley have often seemed ineffectual, willing to paper over serious structural problems in the economy and the society with reassuring but empty slogans and promises.

I witnessed the government in action when I met with a series of officials before the Cornwall College event to try to get a review of the environmental assessment of my family land. They had made it virtually impossible to develop under environmental laws by arbitrarily designating all of it as wetlands.

All I was asking the government bureaucrats was that they actually take a look to see for themselves which portions of the land needed to be protected and which should be left unencumbered — which really was at least seventy-five percent of the land. But at every turn I was running into that bureaucratic nightmare combination of red tape and indifference. Part of my determination came from the fact that I knew that if I had been, say, a white American businessman offering the government a possibility of a new development on the Island, doors would have quickly opened, studies been carried out, and the issue been quickly resolved in favour of the developer. But there was still an air of neo-colonialism to Jamaica, the same kind of attitude that drove Conny from the country in the 1950s when the Frome company bureaucrats were tossed into a tizzy at even the thought that the British-born Mr. Quayle might be offended by an offhand remark. To the Jamaican bureaucrats, I was seen as another homeboy asking for service — and therefore of little value or interest to them.

Thankfully, the trip and my confidence in Jamaica were revived by the Cornwall College event. The ceremony was held off campus at the Half Moon resort, but it was still part of an annual homecoming week that included mentorship programs, a track and field meet, and a soccer game with the school's biggest rival. It was impossible not to be infected by nostalgia for the days when I was living with my Granny Richards on Dome Street and walking up the hill to the school. On my way to the ceremony I drove up to the college, still painted in the school's red and gold colours. The school was largely unchanged from the 1950s, with its coat of arms and motto painted on the walls. It had been situated here, on the hill overlooking the town and the sea, for more than a century. My strongest memories were of the playing field and the pride we felt when we won for the school the first of a string of soccer championships.

Cornwall college told you from the outset: *Disce aut discede*. Learn or leave. Sink or swim. But then on the sporting fields and in your interactions with your fellow students, it taught you the value of teamwork, and you were expected to show solidarity to your classmates. If you made it across after the original command of sink or swim, you were expected to throw a lifeline to the others who were struggling.

Four of us were being inducted into what the college had designated the Men of Might circle, including Kenneth Baugh, a former Jamaican deputy prime minister and foreign affairs minister. According to the simple convention of these ceremonies, someone reads out the highlights of your bio, and you are called to the front of the hall and presented with a plaque. A word of thanks, polite applause, and it is over. The rest of the evening was made up of pleasant banter among the gathered alumni, good food, and, after the presentation, a dance to a band composed mainly of Cornwall alumni.

To a former teacher, an acknowledgement from your own school that you ran the race well means a bit more than it might to most. Now I was eighty years old and, like everyone, a bit incredulous at the march of time. But in my visit to the school earlier in the day I had been surrounded by the next generation of kids, as eager to find a place for themselves in the ever-changing world as we had been. I realized then what this award meant to me. It situated me in the flow of time, from my beginnings to my elder years, with the new generation, the future, going forward into an always new world.

Jan and I arrived back in Toronto in the midst of one of the most intense election campaigns in the country's history, pitting the angry white men and women of the ruling Conservative Party against everyone else. Canada suddenly found itself debating banning the niqab, revoking citizenship, and setting up snitch lines to report on the barbaric cultural practices of immigrants. As it turned out, this was the last, flailing attempt at dog-whistle politics by the dying Harper regime. The country voted for Trudeau the Younger and the Liberals to sweep the Conservatives from power. The Liberals were once again promising to try to do better.

Personally, I had a sign for Linda McQuaig and the New Democratic Party on my lawn in Cabbagetown, but like almost everyone else in the country I was relieved to see the Harper Conservatives gone, and I was hopeful when the new Prime Minister Justin Trudeau named his Cabinet with equal numbers of women and men. He was also proud to have named a number of East Indian, Asian, and Indigenous people to the Cabinet, exclaiming that his Cabinet "looks like Canada!"

I ran into Jean Augustine the next day, and as a lifelong Liberal she was absolutely delighted by the new government and its promising start. I couldn't resist mentioning that I had heard Justin's comment about a Cabinet that looks like Canada but hadn't seen a single Black person behind him at Rideau Hall. Jean scolded me for even mentioning it. It was too early to judge the man — he'd only been elected for a couple of weeks. Just watch him, she said.

I was sceptical about putting too much hope in one man. The culprit or the saviour is never a single person. The problem has never been a lack of good people in the country.

I am happy to say I have known many individual Canadians who stood up for what was right in the world: friends like Ray Scrowpad and Jack Horsley; business associates like Irwin Siderson, Ernie Nock, Bob Buchan, and Gary Slaight; Roy McMurtry and Bill McMurtry, neighbours and friends; and Gordon Cressy, Stephen Lewis, Bill Davis, and many others who stood alongside our community in our demand for justice, and who would never think of discriminating against someone on the basis of race.

But lost to most Canadians during the niqab wars in the run-up to the election campaign was the release of an EKOS poll showing that 46% of Canadians thought there were too many immigrants in Canada, and 41% said there were too many people of colour. That is the bedrock on which the racist foundation is built, and it is still there. We must continue to educate these people and, when they act on their ignorance, to denounce their acts. We must see things as they are if we hope to make them better. But first of all, we have to stop blaming the victims for the misery we create for them.

On the race issue, Canadians still too often reminded me of the student council at Guelph in the mid-1950s, sending sternly worded admonitions to newspapers in the American South regarding the treatment of Blacks, while staying deafeningly silent about the fact that lunch counters in towns down the highway from the campus were off limits to Blacks, and the campus chaplain was telling white girls that they must not go out with Black students.

I recall the motto of another school in Jamaica, where my sister served as principal: *Esse non videri* — to be, and not to seem. As my generation passes the torch, this remains the challenge for Canada. In a way, it remains the challenge for us all and it is how I have tried, with greater or lesser success, to live my own life.

ACKNOWLEDGEMENTS

I imagine that for every book there is a long list of people you need to thank for the help you received along the way. For a memoir, the story of your life, this task is especially daunting. So many people have inspired me and shaped my values and ideas, helped me move ahead in business, or simply offered me their friendship, that it is impossible to thank them all. So I will begin with an apology to those who I have left out.

I cannot begin without thanking my family, my parents Benjamin Augustus Jolly and Ina Euphemia Jolly (née Arthurs) and my brothers and sisters — Barbara, Hyacinth, Desmond, and Winston. Our parents gave all of us happy childhoods where we were taught to work hard and be respectful but with lots of space for us to fill with the joy of growing up in our lively village by the sea.

Both my parents, as I have referred to in the book, inspired me by their example. And in Canada that role was filled by Violet Blackman and Harry Gairey, who fought for a place in Canada for three generations of Blacks and who helped to make our city, Toronto, a place where, finally, we could survive and, at times, thrive.

Among those important in this regard, I have to mention Bromley Armstrong, Al Hamilton, Dudley Laws, Jean Augustine and Fil Fraser, Charles Roach, and Romain Pitt.

In building and running the radio station, I would like to give a special mention to Carl Redhead, Nicole Jolly, Gary Slaight, Bob Buchan, Tony Davy, and all of the talented staff.

In my other business interests, I would like to thank Irwin Siderson, Chris Bhagwat, Flo Brown, Milt Graham, Marion Snow, and again all of the staff.

There are, of course, friends who travelled with me along the way. I have to mention Conny Campbell, Don Parchment, Eric Jolly, and Merrily Weisbord.

In the nuts and bolts of putting this book together I have to thank Peter McFarlane who provided invaluable assistance in shaping the manuscript, my assistant Matthew Gray, editor Peter Norman, ECW Press creative director Crissy Calhoun, and publisher Jack David.

I would also like to give special mention to my children — Nicole, Michael, and Kevin — who have always found new ways to make me proud, to appreciate the present, and hope for the future. They have all been and continue to be blessings. Finally, and this is clearly the case of last but not at all least, I would like to thank my life companion, Janice Williams, who shares my life in every way, and that includes a great deal of help in putting together this book.

APPENDIX

Awards Received

Undated:

Daniel G. Hill Community Service Award

Black History Makers Award

United Achievers' Club of Brampton Community Service Award

Special Award of Merit, Black Business and Professional
Association (BBPA)

Commendation of Excellence, Cornwall College

Onyx Lions Club Outstanding Community Service Award

Appreciation of Service, Grandravine Special Hockey Program

Jamaica National Building Society and The Gleaner Company
Award of Merit

Red Cross Award for Haiti Earthquake Support Presented to

FLOW 93.5

BBPA Award of Appreciation for years of service to Toronto's
Black community

Dated:

1983 Jamaican Canadian Association (JCA) School a Child Run
Award for 2nd Place

1989 Jamaican Canadian Association (JCA) Certificate of
Appreciation in recognition of contribution toward the
acquisition of the JCA Centre

1990 Special Olympics Softball Team Coach Appreciation Award

1992 Commemorative Medal for the 125th anniversary of the
Confederation of Canada

1993–1995 YMCA Council of Advisory Governors Appreciation
Award

1995 African National Congress Certificate of Appreciation
signed by Nelson Mandela

1995 Cornwall College Old Boys Association (Toronto Chapter)
Award of Appreciation and Dedicated Service to the
Caribbean Community

1996 Black Business Professional Association (BBPA) Harry
Jerome Award of Merit

1998 African Canadian Achievement Award (Business)

1998 Black Action Defence Committee Award of Honour

1999 Jamaican Canadian Association Award of Recognition and
Commitment

2000 Award of Excellence in Recognition of Black History

2001 Canadian Urban Music Awards Special Achievement Award

2001 City of Toronto Job Fair and Career Exposition
Appreciation Award (Presented to FLOW 93.5)

2002 Toronto Study Group Lifetime Achievement Award

2002 Queen's Golden Jubilee Medal

2002 National Association of Black Female Executives in Music and Entertainment (NABFEME) Award of Appreciation

2003 Black Action Defence Committee President's Award

2003 Daphne DaCosta Award for outstanding contributions (Cancer awareness and prevention)

2005 The University of Toronto Black Alumni Association Honorary Alumni Award

2005 Metro Fay Award of Appreciation Presented to FLOW 93.5

2005 CAB | ARC (Canadian Association of Broadcasters/ Association canadienne des radiodiffuseurs) Gold Ribbon Award presented to FLOW 93.5 for Community Services – Anti-Violence Campaign

2005 Ontario Association of Broadcasters Community Service Award Presented to FLOW 93.5 for Anti-violence Campaign

2007 Consulate General of Jamaica Award of Appreciation

2007 African Canadian Achievement Award for Excellence in Media

2007 No. 42 Division Award of Appreciation for Contribution to 10th Annual Community Police Picnic, Presented to FLOW 93.5

2008 Canadian Urban Institute's Urban Leadership City Soul Award

2008 Birth of Paradise Award for outstanding contribution in the field of business development

2009 BBPA (Black Business Professional Association), EFCCC (Educational Foundation for Children's Care Canada) and Metro Fay Award of Recognition for ongoing sponsorship of the Annual Martin Luther King Celebration

2010 BBPA Award of Dedication and Contribution

2011 African Canadian Achievement Award of Excellence

2012 Queen Elizabeth II Diamond Jubilee Medal

2012 Caribbean Tales Honour Award for outstanding
contribution to Black people in media

2013 Ontario Black History Society Dr. Anderson Abbott Award
for High Achievement

2014 Cornwall College Old Boys Association (CCOBA)
Canadian Chapter Recognition Award

2015 Cornwall College "Men of Might" Award

Sporting Awards:

1953 Cornwall College – Olivier Shield Champion

1979 Parkway South Tennis Club Singles Runner-up Award

1979 Parkway South Tennis Club Doubles Winner

1980 Parkway South Tennis Club Singles Runner-up Award

1980 Parkway South Tennis Club Doubles Winner

1981 Parkway South Tennis Club Men's Doubles Runner-up,
D. Jolly & B. Sutton

1982 Parkway South Tennis Club Men's Doubles Winners,
D. Jolly & B. Sutton

*List of Organizations that Mr. Jolly is involved with and has
been involved with throughout the years:*

Black Business Professional Association (Founder)

Harry Jerome Scholarship Fund (Founder)

Harry Jerome Awards (Founder)

The Jamaican Canadian Association (Treasurer)

Black Action Defense Committee (Founding Member)

Committee for Due Process (Founding Member)

Daphne Dacosta Cancer Association (Member)

Jane and Finch Concerned Citizens Movement (Member)

Black Inmates Organization (Member)

Harriett Tubman Games (Co-Founder)

YMCA - Central Toronto (Board of Governors)

Surrey Place Centre, Toronto (Board Member)

Ontario Nursing Home Association (Membership Committee)

Caribana (Special Committee Member)

PACE – Project for the Advancement of Childhood Education (Member and Sponsor)

Advisory Board for Toronto Mayor's Economic Competitiveness Committee 2006-2008 (Board Member)

Toronto International Film Festival Group 2005-2008 (Board of Directors)

CaribbeanTales 2011 – present (Board of Directors)

GET THE EBOOK FREE!